PSYCHIC MEDIUM WITHIN

The story of my awakening – and the beginning of yours

ED CARLTON

AUTHORS PLACE
—PRESS—

Published by Authors Place Press
9885 Wyecliff Drive, Suite 200
Highlands Ranch. CO 80126
AuthorsPlace.com

Page 59 (chakra picture) Copyright © byPeter Hermes Furian
Page 80 (psychic breath) Copyright © by Miro Kovacevic
Page 96 (color wavelengths) Copyright © by Mila Gligoric

Manufactured in the United States of America.

ISBN: 978-1-62865-664-0

CONTENTS

CHAPTER 6

Healing with Energy as a Medium 54

CHAPTER 7

Developing your Psychic Abilities 72

CHAPTER 8

Empowering the Empath Within 86

CHAPTER 9

Conclusion - Awakening energy and daily routine 104

"The wound is the place where the light enters you."

-Rumi

"If you change the way you look at things,
the things you look at change."

-Wayne Dyer

A special thanks to:

Julie Smith, for helping me edit my first draft.

Koko Zamoyski, my incredible writing mentor and dearest friend, for helping me believe in myself and creating a writer out of me. You are truly an Earth Angel and a blessing.

My sisters, Sonya and Leslie. My parents. Dad, you showed me what true strength is. Mom, you have always believed in me, even when I have dreamt the impossible. I could not have survived without you.

My son, Jaiden. You saved my life just by coming into it. You teach me the beauty and wonder of the world every day.

And lastly, my Partner, Patrick. I have always said you are my hero. You have stuck by my side when most wouldn't. You are kind, loyal and the greatest friend anyone could have. Our lives have changed so dramatically, but you are my constant. You are my rock.

This is a story in two parts.

The first part is about my journey of discovery…*that I am* a Psychic/Medium.

In the second part I share my recommendations and insights, in the hope of assisting you in unlocking your psychic abilities – should you desire to do so.

Namasté,

Ed Carlton

PREFACE

Life has a way of throwing us curve balls. These surprises can be frustrating until we get to the point on our life path where we can see (or hope to see) the larger picture – and understand that those surprises serve a purpose.

All my life I have heard these interesting sayings: "What doesn't kill you makes you stronger." And, "Nothing happens to you, it happens for you." I remember pondering how crazy these sounded, because they were usually attached to something harsh – something I didn't ask for and didn't want.

Life is full of ironies. "Someone" up there has a strange sense of humor. It's definitely hard to see the big picture – especially when we're living in it. Before I turned 30, if someone had told me I would write a book I'd have said that person was crazy. I grew up with a reading comprehension problem and sometimes was left feeling shy and not quite so smart as the others.

Then I started growing in my psychic abilities and began to find my path of enlightenment. After that I no longer let those old beliefs define me. Ironically, though, if someone had told me I was a Psychic and would end up practicing professionally, I expect I'd have called the psych ward to pick that person up.

Yes, there was a time when I didn't even know if I believed in psychics. Like most people in our society, I had a misconception of what a psychic is. I still held the misconception that a psychic was a scammer, or someone practicing spells or reading your future in a crystal ball – yet when I was overtaken by a 'vision' I did not freeze.

My father still has his doubts, and still refers to me as a fortuneteller. If I were, I could get the lottery numbers. (That's just cliché, of course, but that's what I believed, and I think most people have that perception.) Society is changing, though. We are expanding our consciousness and opening our minds to the possibility that there is more. The amazing thing I have discovered through my journey – studying and reading, and then teaching – is that all of us have psychic abilities. We have simply misunderstood them. Or mislabeled them.

I was a sensitive child. My emotions were heightened. I would never have thought that was the unskilled aspect of my psychic empathic abilities. I was labeled as dramatic, emotional, extreme – even hypochondriac. And when my abilities took over, my life became unstable.

*

Being a psychic is not a job. It is a calling. I feel it in every fiber of my being. To be a psychic is to understand that there is so much—much more than anyone can possibly imagine. Our reality is like a rubber band. Just when I think I understand what is on the other side, my consciousness expands and stretches to a whole new reality. It amazes me that there is no limit to the possibilities.

When I accepted the calling as a psychic and teacher, I became a way-shower. Situations in life happen to groups of people. We shift together. Because I am a way-shower, situations happen to me a month or two ahead of my clients and students. By then I can understand, have learned to deal with the situation, so clients and students come to me and I can provide tools they need for understanding.

Here's a sample situation. It may seem that in all my relationships—with friends and some family members—there's anger. They get angry and create fights. For what seems no reason, everything becomes extremely dramatic. This may happen because Spirit is using this way to provide clearness for those in toxic relationships. They are just becoming aware of the fact. They become very emotional and cannot see the situation clearly. At that point I can be of help, because I've been through something similar.

I write this book to tell my personal story of acceptance and growth, and also to aid your growth. In explaining my journey, I offer teachings you can tap – and thereby discover your true nature and understand your own abilities. There is much more than most people can imagine. I want to help you feel the connection and see the bigger picture – and come to understand who you are truly meant to be.

CHAPTER 1

NEW LIFE: MY JOURNEY TO BECOMING AN EMPATH

WHEN I WAS SIX, I found out I was going to die and I was devastated. I was told it was because of something called "Original Sin." What does that even mean to a six-year-old? I was raised in a very religious family. I went to a private Catholic school, which required mass every day before school started. We all sat there because we were required to, though we didn't really understand most of what was said. I hated seeing that "poor naked man" with the sad, compassionate eyes (something I now relate to very well) looking up, nailed to a cross. The three intertwined vines with thorns pierced the flesh causing the droplets of blood to become visible. It always pained me to see that. What was worse later was being told he had died for me. That was devastating. I didn't want anyone to die for me. I didn't ask him to. I remember wondering why we were celebrating his death and not his life? (Something I still wonder about.)

Later on, while attending Catholic school, I was told I was going to hell after I died. Why? Because I was gay. It didn't matter that I was a good person, wanting never to hurt anyone, and living a good life. I was told not to question God, because God doesn't make mistakes. Well, he had made a mistake with me. He made me gay, and then I felt condemned and I suffered because I was different. I didn't know then how different I was, but it wasn't because I was gay. As I matured, no matter how hard I tried, I could not get the self-love back that was taken from me at such a young age.

I realize now that my personal crisis of self-condemnation was the impetus for my discovery years later – a journey which confirmed that there is great Love, not just for me, but for all, regardless of orientation. The Source Creator, or what most people refer to as God, has created and given us extraordinary gifts hidden within us. These gifts may not be revealed until we intentionally search for our true Self – and that search may be triggered by suffering.

Though I was triggered to search for the expression of my psychic gifts through suffering that may not necessarily be so with others. Whatever the circumstance, know that within you there is a doorway to your psychic self, your True Self. By sharing my story, it is my hope and intention to assist you in your journey to Awakening – finding your gifts and spiritual abilities and discovering your True Self.

*

My mother knew I was different the moment I was born. You see, my mother has psychic abilities, but like a lot of people, for most of her life she suppressed her abilities. Society has a way of condemning those different from the norm. I was considered strange or "very sensitive." The very first time she held me my mother knew I was gay, but she kept it to herself. She wanted to allow me to discover my own identity. What I discovered was not the effect of being gay, but rather a greater gift.

I had an unusually heightened sense of hearing, smell and taste – was sensitive to certain foods, emotions, and even touch. I could feel the energy coming off tangible things, including plants and people. I remember my mother asking me to tell her what was going on with my sisters. She knew I could 'read' them.

This unique sensitivity was mine because I am an "Empath" – which means I experience the energy of life around me and maybe even experience the feelings and emotions of another person, or in some cases take on another person's physical pain. Just think what kind of mental and emotional confusion that causes for a person in the early stages of life.

At a glance you'd say I had a typical childhood. It is taught in the spiritual community that before we are born, we choose our parents (as our parents choose us). This is considered a type of "soul contract." We choose them because on a soul level they can teach us many lessons in this lifetime. There were attributes and lessons I needed to learn through having this particular family. I encourage you to take a moment to reflect upon the gifts given by these close relationships, especially the hard ones.

My dad retired from the Air Force, a Chief Master Sergeant. Though I love my dad dearly, he was my greatest challenge. He epitomized strength, loved competitive sports and was passionate about politics, with a deep commitment to community. He tried very hard to instill these attributes in me. I was eight when my father enrolled my older sister and me in soccer. He thought it would be a wonderful team-building experience and a way to get to know some of the community. What father doesn't want the son to be a prize-winning athlete? My older sister was a natural, very athletic. She ran to and fro with the ball right where it needed to be. I, on the other hand, was enthralled by the energy coming off the flowers in the field. They were mesmerizing. I lay on the ground and picked the dandelions, a heavenly experience until everyone in the stands and my father started yelling at me as the ball and players neared me. That was the end of my soccer career. (I wasn't too devastated.)

My father didn't give up. He enrolled me in T-ball. The intense energy of the ball panicked me and I could never hit it or catch it. After many frustrations caused by my failures in sports, my dad turned to me one day in the car and said, "Let's stop playing." I was so relieved, but at the same time sadly thought, '*We can forget bonding.*' Truth was, Dad and I had little in common.

For years, I thought I would never live up to his expectations and continually felt like I let him down. Empaths are people pleasers, and I tried in every way I knew to please him. When I stopped trying to please, our relationship became awkward.

I was twenty-one when I discovered that love is accepting, strong – and not defined by gender. When I turned twenty-one, I came out to my folks that I was gay. Mom already knew, but my dad really surprised me. He was relieved – not so much to learn that I was gay, but so long as I had been holding on to my 'secret,' he had been holding on to his. He had thought he was at fault for the awkwardness in our relationship. When he gathered the understanding that it was not, he accepted me for who I was. His son. He loved me – and remained his authentic self, which allowed me to develop into my authentic self. This is a prime example of true strength and true love.

HIDING

My parents worked hard to make sure we always had the necessities of life. They believed in education. They raised three children and earned their master's degrees. We have been through a lot together and I am very proud to call them my family. We are a family that sticks together and are always there for one another. When going through a spiritual transformation, loving support is a blessing, and I was greatly blessed. If you're one who does not have a close family, be aware that a network of like-minded friends can also serve as a perfect support.

In my youth I tried very hard to fit in with the other kids, but never did. I had a good group of friends, but strangely, I knew things the other kids didn't know. I always felt different from the others because I *felt more* than the others did –things such as what they were feeling inside. I did not speak of these things. I could also *feel* the energy coming off plants and animals.

I was young and didn't understand these feelings, so I struggled with my identity and relationships. Later on, I learned that though most Empaths do have friends, they often feel secluded and alone.

It's true that I was living with a secret. I didn't know why I had this ability to tune into the energy around me. It confused me, sometimes frightened me. I was fortunate that I was able to talk with my mom about these things. She listened without judgment. I remember crying one night and saying, "I know this person doesn't like me." She asked if the person said something or acted a certain way that caused me to think so. "No," I told her – and added that somehow I just knew.

At that time few people even knew there was such a thing as an Empath, but my mother knew I had a 'special gift' – like hers, though she denied it. And then when I was in my teens, something extraordinary happened and fractured my sense of self. I experienced a paradigm shift that triggered a defensive shutdown of my psychic center and a refusal of my empathic gifts. This locked me into a state of denial for many years.

My older sister was a rebellious teenager. I was not. With her adept manipulation skills, one night after curfew she convinced me to sneak out of the house. As the fates would have it, my mother caught me. That extraordinary shift I mentioned, a paradigm shift, occurred as two powerful emotions surged through me when my mother caught me. I was seized by the heart and scared into immobility, and suddenly realized that the powerful emotions I was feeling were not my feelings – but hers! Inside me, I felt her heart-breaking disappointment.

It was like my consciousness was in her. I could feel the pain I caused her. This kind of experience may be a common right-of-passage for many teenagers, but most do not feel what their parent is feeling. I was hugely aware that what I was feeling was not 'normal.'

My mother is a caring and forgiving person, so after a long discussion and some duly earned punishment, all was forgiven on her end. It was in that moment that I knew why some people call this gift "super" natural. It sure left me feeling super different. She forgave me, of course, but the experience slammed me.

How could I feel what someone else was feeling?! It wasn't normal, I thought – so I doubted my sanity. I reacted by shutting down inside and not caring. If I could focus only on the surface of life, I wouldn't have to be in touch with that hidden part of me – or so I thought. By the time I hit my twenties I had only one focus: having fun!!

I became a flight attendant for a major airline, made new friends and traveled around the world. Sounds like a wonderful life, huh? Those were some of the best days of my life and some wonderful friends supported me, but inside I felt hollow. I was deeply lonely. I would later learn that many Empaths endure this kind of separation from others – before they master their ability.

I was never good at dating, especially being gay and an Empath. I was too sensitive to others and too uncomfortable in myself. I felt awkward, still holding inside 'my secret.' And like many who are unable to bear the weight of secrets, I started drinking – but I was a lightweight and after a few drinks would get sick. About that same time, I began having weight issues because I was eating to fill the void of loneliness, then suddenly got concerned about the weight gain and stopped eating. So then I was underweight, extremely underweight, and began to experiment with drugs to fill the void, but nothing assuaged my sense of separation. And nothing filled the loneliness inside.

I confess these things so you know you are not alone in the battle for self-acceptance. This negating self – before self-discovery, is common. Until our feelings and truths are recognized and honed, hidden psychic gifts can and likely will distort our view of life.

During this time, I began having minor back pain that became more and more frequent. I didn't think too much about it at first because both my father and mother had back problems, so I figured mine must be genetic. I thought all I needed was a chiropractor to adjust me. Heck, I was young! I could deal with it.

No matter what else was going on I still suffered the emotional pain of feeling so separated from others. The need to fill the void grew more and more powerful so I took on a project to distract me from my problems. I purchased an old house thinking I could renovate it slowly. My thought was that it was a good idea to keep my mind busy. Looking back, it all sounds crazy: "I'm lonely, and I have back problems—let's renovate an old house. Yup, sounds like a perfect solution…"

I didn't realize I was so desperate to avoid my reality – the reality that I do feel other people's feelings on a deep level. I hold them within my body. I know their feelings before they even tell me. And sometimes I confuse their feelings with my own. And sometimes I am so overwhelmed with feelings that it just hurts to breathe. *That reality*. Since I didn't want to face that reality, I'd just get busy, fix up an old house.

As I write this, Spirit smiles at me. You may ask what I mean. Well, Spirit has many names: the Great Spirit, the Holy Spirit, the Divine, the Holy. Let's just say that Spirit is an essence of the Divine.

As I neared the completion of the renovations, I was in so much pain I had to have back surgery. And then had to have another one. The suffering caused me to stop and look at my life, to question my decision to deny and hide from that 'secret' part of me. After all, it was a major, though silent, part of who I was.

I had to get 'it' off my back, so out of desperation I decided to open myself up to life again – stop hiding and begin the process of self-acceptance. It is often through crisis that we begin our spiritual journey.

At the point when we commit ourselves to our journey of self-discovery, Spirit may give us a gift, a kind of "Atta boy!" to manifest evidence that the journey is the right one. I was found by Love. It was a return to Life and the beginning of my salvation. It was at once a safety net and the springboard to Who I Would Become…a psychic medium, committed to doing Spirit's work.

I AM FOUND BY LOVE

I met Patrick some years back. At the time, he was with someone else and so was I. We worked for the same airlines, though in different capacities. Our paths crossed several times at work throughout that year. He was handsome and quiet and I could feel his depth. It intrigued me, but it seemed to me that we were on different tracks. Several times, in the months that followed, we met coincidentally. It was on the subway, after returning from a flight, that I found out he had broken up with his partner and moved to Philadelphia, where I lived, and another time after a flight we shared drinks with some friends. Neither time did he express any interest in me, and though I was no longer in a relationship, he was not responsive to any of my overtures. I must admit, though, that my expressions of interest were clumsy and awkward. To be honest, I flirted like a teenage girl. It was all extremely awkward and embarrassing for me – sometimes a fluster, a self-conscious flush or a suppressed giggle. That awkwardness caused me to stop trying.

More than once I've been asked why I did not have 'psychic feelings' about Patrick during this time, and I just have to admit that even now I cannot 'read' him. I think that's because as a Free Will Being, I have lessons to learn through the consequences of 'choice.' It's whether the consequence of choice is from a place of Spirit or from the lower 'ego' that determines its effect on our life – and thus the lesson. We all have a right to our privacy, so maybe we shouldn't know some things about our partners. Now that I think about it, very likely one of the reasons I was drawn to him was the "silence" in my emotional field. Some of my friends who are psychics pick up on their partners, but apparently I choose not to. Most of the details I've "picked up" I simply learned through years of being with him.

At my back-pain's peak and just after my second surgery, getting involved in any kind of relationship was the furthest thing from my mind. I was standing in line at the pharmacy in pain and misery, looking as if I had been dragged there…and Patrick appeared. He was happy to see me and wanted to talk, but I hadn't showered because of the surgery and was dressed like patchwork and in so much pain I could not be responsive. I quickly picked up my pain pills and left, thinking I'd never hear from him again. A week passed. An unknown number showed up on my cell phone. It was Patrick. We decided to meet for lunch. I learned a great deal on that one date. Because of all I had been through, there was not even a thought of playing "the game." It was such a relief. We were both honest and 'real' – just being our selves with no pretense, and quickly became fast friends. We laughed and talked for hours. Neither of us wanted that time to end.

Turned out it was an 8-hour date. We walked for miles through the city, and though my pain began increasing I did not want to leave him. One of the first things we learned was that we are both tea drinkers, which is not common among my friends, so we stopped for tea. We were also both voracious readers and, great surprise! – we both cited Harry Potter as our favorite book. Who would have guessed that two adult men would have chosen that book?!

In this transformative state of revelation, we shared our beliefs, hopes, goals, and dreams for the future. Though we didn't agree in every way, there was a feeling that we had been together before and were already connected…already deep friends. And how did we get to love, you ask? How did I know I loved him? We saw each other several times that week. On a cold but beautiful Philadelphia night Patrick and I were walking, just ambling, then he took my hand. It was a marvelous feeling of warmth and closeness. Then suddenly, in the distance, we saw two men approaching.

One of them was my ex-boyfriend. As they came closer Patrick jerked his hand away. It was an uncomfortable moment. As they passed by we exchanged polite "hellos." After that neither of us spoke until we arrived at his apartment where we sat down to talk. I looked into his eyes. They were direct and wide and I saw a tear well up and fall. I asked, "Why are you upset?" I will never forget his response: "I never want to hurt you, or to let you down. I'm afraid I did that by withdrawing my hand from yours when I saw them." At that instant, I knew I loved him, and I knew he loved me. This strong, stoic, quiet man opened himself to my gaze and judgment. A man with a pure heart. A man worthy of loving who made me feel worthy of being loved.

At that time, of course, neither of us could know that I would be going through an intense spiritual transformation in the years ahead. I can say now that I doubt, I would have survived the spiritual metamorphosis required of me if Patrick had not been with me, loving me, believing in me, and using the strength that comes from a pure and loyal heart to sustain our family. The road ahead would test us both.

A PATH APPEARS

Over the next few years my pain subsided but did not go away. I dealt with it and thought my life good. Patrick and I were happy. I experienced moments when it was essential that I spend time alone, secluding myself from everyone. I told Patrick I had to recharge my batteries. In this way, I thought I was managing my 'secret' – the constant emotional push and pull of everyone in my environment, which often exhausted me. It was useless to try to explain it to Patrick because I still didn't understand it myself.

We adopted a baby boy, Jaiden. We seemed to be a happy family, but I had bottled up my empathic abilities for so long I was like a pressure cooker. So of course – the lid blew off! Emotions and pain (physical and emotional) boiled over. You must understand that these were not just my emotions or pain. Remember, Empaths absorb the emotions and pains of others. I was "bottling" all those feelings up, not allowing them to be released. How does someone release something they don't know they're holding? We humans do hold things in our body on a subconscious and energetic level – and often have no idea we are doing so.

The ensuing changes happened fast – and ultimately would alter my life completely. I spiraled into a deep depression. The physical pain I experienced can hardly be described. I went through five more years of chronic pain and six more back surgeries. During that time, I took morphine four times a day, had three spinal injections per year, and endured countless hours of physical therapy, acupuncture and a plethora of medication. It was all just unimaginable. The doctors called it "pain management." Yes, managing the pain, yet still unable to determine the cause. As a result, I was bedridden for two years. Imagine what this did to my "happy family" with a new baby boy. The medications changed me, and I became unlike myself. It was killing my spirit. And I hit rock bottom fast.

You might wonder what caused all these back problems. Well, from a "normal" standpoint, nothing. I didn't have a major car accident, I wasn't in some huge fight, didn't jump out of a burning building. My Empath abilities caused all my back problems. I want you to think of emotions. I want you to think of the hardest time of your life. Do you remember that time? Do you remember how you felt? You felt heavy. Now multiply that by thousands. That is what happened to me. Some feelings are heavy. They weigh on our body. An Empath sometimes absorbs other people's emotions. I did that for 30 years times thousands of others' pains and sadness. All that was happening on the subconscious level, but the weight of it caused my body to break down.

I believe that Spirit/God puts people in our life for a reason, so it was obvious why Patrick was brought to me. Patrick was the rock on which I was able to rebuild the foundation of my new life. He is my rock.

He loves me. He is also logical and balanced, so he kept me grounded through my emotional chaos. And his spiritual side, not the psychic spiritual, but the part that believes in a higher power, allowed me to seek Spirit without judgment. He provided the perfect ballast for me, and he also had the strength to support our family financially, while taking care of our child and me. Sometimes, when he grew tired, his understanding and compassion would sway. Those times were especially hard on us, for when someone you love is suffering there is definitely a toll to be paid. I suffered. He suffered. I have learned through my readings that if a change is needed in our life and we don't allow it, Spirit will step in – and when Spirit steps in it's likely going to be in a big and dramatic way.

So yes, Spirit stepped in, and it was big. Suddenly, Patrick was promoted. The promotion required us to move to the other side of the state, far from where my parents lived. They had helped us so much with our son during this stressful time and now we had to move to a place where we didn't know anyone. What we did know was that something had to change in our lives, so we decided to look at this forced move as opportunity, as blessing.

The movers packed, we loaded up the car with the animals and our child, and we started the journey. We were a half-hour away from our new place when I turned to Patrick and said, "I can't do this anymore. We are being given a chance for a new life and I feel dead. I can't live like this for the rest of my life. We have tried everything. I don't know what else to do. All I know is I can't live like this. There has to be a reason God has given me this pain. I can't take it anymore. I don't know what, but something has to be done."

At the time I didn't realize how profoundly that prayer (or plea) would affect my life. Spirit heard and helped – and because of the move I got a new doctor and a new pain specialist. I told them both I was going off the medication. They thought I was crazy and wanted to know what my alternate plan was. Truth was, I didn't have one, but I got them to agree to slowly reduce the medication. And then I did what every person in this age of technology who's looking for an answer does. I searched the Internet. I looked online for alternative ways to reduce chronic pain. Chiropractic, tried it. Acupuncture, tried it. Herbs, hmm, maybe… keep looking. Magic, hmm…that's extreme, haven't tried that, not really sure I'm into that…wait…look—an herb shop that sells magic stuff, a metaphysical store. And only a couple miles away.

CHAPTER 2

A DOOR OPENS

THE EMPORIUM WAS A simple shop, but the owner was anything but. I remember walking in and seeing a formidable woman with jet-black hair. I could 'feel' her empathically. She was a woman beyond extraordinary. I felt a fire within her soul that I knew could spark the hidden talents in even a mediocre student. I also felt she would not be taken lightly. I was reminded that even as fire illuminates, it burns.

She politely explained the shop to me, while continuing her work. That day I bought books on magic, meditation, chakras, oils, herbs, and developing psychic abilities. I sat there for hours reading the cover of the books trying to remember what I had researched online, and interrupted the store owner at least a dozen times to get her advice. You name it and I bought it. I was willing to try anything and almost everything. I also purchased guided meditation CDs and candles. After I checked out, the fiery lady said they offered classes and put in my hand a handout about upcoming ones. One thing I knew was that if she was teaching the classes, I was there! She was awesome! I felt I had been guided there, as if she had been waiting for me.

I dove into my research and tried everything. Some things stuck, most did not. I noticed most had one thing in common: they all spoke of Divine Power (also referred to as Spirit) and the Power of Intention. I came to understand that Divine Power has given a unique piece of itself to us, which we call our soul, our spirit, our light, our divine self.

Divine Power has given us a soul with unique qualities. These qualities are directly from the Source – or God. Since all these qualities come from the same Source, they are all connected, and this is how we as people can connect psychically. Each soul is unique as well as each psychic power, and all souls come from the same Source. Therefore they (or should I say we?) are all connected, which means we can connect with each other and other spirits.

After months of research it was time to put what I'd learned into practice, so I started the offered classes. That fiery lady became my first teacher. She taught many metaphysical classes, including methods of basic spiritual protection, and also herbs, chakras, auras, angels, divination and developing psychic abilities, and meditation—just to name a few. What I learned from books and from online research was affirmed in these classes. She and I became friends, but she was more than that – she was a mentor. And I expect by now that you've picked up on the fact that I was hungry (you could say ravenous) for knowledge and experience.

The protection class was particularly helpful. You might ask, "From what does one need protection?" Well, if you're an Empath, the answer is, "Many things." You need to know how to "shield" yourself from picking up and absorbing other people's emotions or feelings. This portion of her teaching was what I was most needing. Once I learned how to release other people's emotions and shield myself, I felt I was on the right path and was ready to accept my gifts.

My back pain, though, was still there. Was I being sidetracked with this spiritual seeking? I tried many modalities and nothing helped. The hardest thing I tried was meditation. Basically, the purpose of meditation is to turn your mind off, stop thinking—and just be in the moment… allowing yourself to listen to the stillness. It sounds easy but takes years of practice and patience. Eventually though, you experience pure bliss.

One day I decided to combine meditation with what I had learned about the chakra system. (I'll explain about chakras in another chapter). When I combined them, I could feel the healing taking place – because finally I'd discovered a method of relieving the back pain.

The more I meditated with my new chakra 'color method,' the more relief I felt. I began to reduce further the amount of medication I was taking and put my focus on learning to trust my intuition and my feelings. I spent hours of meditating with the colors, finding a sense of peace and calm I had never before experienced. The colors grew into something more than just simple colors. They started to have intelligence, warmth, kindness, compassion and love. This all probably sounds crazy, but as the colors in my meditations grew and expanded, the healing of my back pain became evident – and eventually became tolerable.

The change was dramatic and set my life on track. Finally, I could help out, *and* enjoy my family again – a relief for us all. And finally, the day came when I was able to get off my medical leave and go back to work as a flight attendant.

One time I spent an entire layover in a meditation with the colors, and when I got home was in a euphoric state of peace. The next morning Patrick picked me up from the airport and I began describing to him what I was so vividly seeing. I saw orange, red and yellow-gold in his aura. The sky that day was a clear light blue, but I saw shades of pink in the blue. Though Patrick couldn't see the pink, I knew the pink was love surrounding the earth. It was the most incredible thing! Though I haven't seen that since, I know it's there. I remember telling Patrick, "I know I sound crazy and if this is crazy I never want to go back. This is the happiest I have ever been in my life." The sense of bliss was overwhelming.

The experience of the colors began slowing down, only appearing in meditation, and seemed to have a life of their own. For months I just watched them and they became clearer and clearer in each meditation. They began to make themselves known as angels. These angels did not look like the 'cute people with wings' displayed at my mom's house. These angels looked like streaks of energy. Initially, I was skeptical. Maybe this was all happening in my head. How could I be sure?

The angels communicated with me in a way I knew very well: feeling. I felt it with every fiber of my being, with every emotion, with all my Empathic abilities. I had spent most of my life struggling to understand, 'Why me? Why do I have to deal with everyone else's emotions and feelings?' Now it finally made sense. I could actually *feel* the pure love! *I could feel it!* For the first time I knew why I was chosen to be an Empath. I knew that my struggle with other people's emotions, and enduring all of that long back pain, had led me to this moment. I was suddenly humbled and understood that I had been given a gift – and in discovering the gift, I knew I had a responsibility.

I could feel the Divine Light inside me. My soul and spirit exhaled. The insight was stunning and sudden. I knew I was supposed to help other people connect with their own spirit/soul. When we connect with our spirit/soul, the entire world changes and we start to sense the spiritual world all around us. When we connect with our own spirit, our abilities enhance (or manifest). We sense God within everything and everyone. God/Source had given me a gift and a responsibility, which meant I had to learn how to use it.

BECOMING

One by one, Angels and Guides came forth to introduce themselves. Eventually pictures and images started appearing in my mind, and sometimes the pictures were symbolic. These symbolic pictures were often repeated and I worked together with Spirit to create a sort of Symbol dictionary, a communication resource between me and the Angels and Guides. I worked with my angels and guides to understand their messages and effectively communicate with them as they provided information from Spirit.

I soon realized that every person has a symbol dictionary or communication dictionary. During my meditations, I asked many questions – questions I like to call the "big ones." What are we? What is the soul? What is the purpose of this life? It was explained that this life is meant to be full of lessons and discovery. Every lesson or challenge that we face in life, we choose before we are born. This is called our "soul contract" and these challenges and discoveries help our soul grow and deepen, and in doing so we become closer to God. The closer we are to God, the more elevated our vision, the more harmonious our lives become. We can even enter a state of Bliss.

Our angels and guides want to help us reach that blissful point, but they cannot intervene – because we have free will. We must ask for their assistance, and then they can help guide us. Spirit will nudge us in the direction that will provide the most growth but will not make the choice for us. It's our life to live, our lesson to learn. I continued to work hard and study. I was spending a lot of time with my angels and guides – and enjoying my family. It seemed my life couldn't get better. This is normally where the other shoe drops, but not this time.

It is interesting to note, that I am one who does not care for schedules or rules. I have never considered myself a disciplined person. As much as I enjoy meditation, it would not have been an essential practice for me, but as I proceeded I found that if I don't meditate regularly, the back pain starts to creep back in – so I gladly meditate. I have come to know that it is Spirit's way of telling me, "It's time to check in."

I built a strong foundation with my angels and guides, and my life at home was good. My partner and I were solid, our son was happy, and we were finally financially stable. I continued to grow. My next step was just waiting for me to catch up.

CHAPTER 3

BECOMING MORE

I was amazed with my life and thought things couldn't get any better, when during one of my meditations a 60-year-old lady came to me. She was barely walking with a couple teeth missing, wild gray hair and a very prominent chin. Her smile was beautiful and so kind. It was my Grandmother. I wondered why she had appeared. Then her voice came through my mind. She was here to help me on the next part of my journey to becoming a Medium.

I am asked quite often what the difference is between a psychic and a medium. You must be a psychic to be a medium, but not every psychic is a medium. A psychic reads the *energy* of the other person. A medium communicates directly with a spirit. I've talked to many psychics and mediums and few ever agree on the answer to the question, "Can any psychic be a medium?" I personally think that every psychic can become a medium. Everything is energy – and energy is all about vibration and frequency, but mediumship deals with another level of energy. Interfacing at this level requires learning how to "tune in" to the frequency – or vibration, of the spiritual being.

I didn't know anything about being a "medium." I had seen a couple of TV shows featuring 'mediums,' but when my grandmother appeared, the skeptic in me took over. I told Maw-Maw – that's what we called her, "If you are real, then you have to prove it. Tell me something I don't know, something I can confirm with my mom.

And she did. She sent me memories and feelings of my mother's childhood at the age of seven. My mother was the oldest of three, and the younger ones both brothers. Her father was not around much, but my grandmother loved him dearly. She would always take him back when he showed up. My mother felt she had to be a responsible adult at age eight. She cared for her two younger brothers. She always felt like my grandmother favored the boys – and that's what my grandmother shared with me.

She showed me what their New Orleans home looked like. The entrance door to their place had large glass panes that went half way down the door. I saw the layout of the place. In the meditation, I walked into a large hall that went the length of the house, with the living room off to the side. Continuing down the hall I saw the dining room, kitchen and then the bedroom. My grandmother told me she worked at a hospital that was close by, that she used to walk to work and how much she enjoyed her job. Then, to my surprise, the scene switched. I saw my great-uncle sitting at a table with Maw-Maw. They were playing cards. While my great-aunt sat and listened to them tease each other, I could actually *feel* the dynamics of their relationship. I watched as they interacted.

I knew that if this wasn't real, I must have an amazing imagination. Through it all, I could feel my grandmother's love for me. It was overwhelming. I could feel how proud she was, and I started to cry.

After I steadied my emotions, I called my mother. I knew she would be at work, but I had to call her immediately, even if just to leave a message. She answered the phone! Said she had felt that she needed the day off and so she took it. (See how Spirit works, if you listen?) I told her all that Maw-Maw had shared with me and she confirmed all the visions and memories my grandmother gave me during my meditation. She confirmed the relationship between her and her mother, all of which I did not know. The two of us cried joyfully.

For the next couple months, every time I went into meditation my uncles, aunts, cousins, and friends of the family appeared. Each time, I'd call my mother and she would confirm all of it. I had never experienced anything like it before. I had a hard time believing it…but I was becoming a medium.

I went back to my favorite metaphysical shop and the owner recommended that I see a psychic. You may ask, Why? Because I have found that the hardest thing for me is to be a clear channel for myself. Personal emotions distort clear discernment of what Spirit is communicating – so I was directed to the back room of the shop.

I was in for a treat. There I met a woman with a personality that stood ten feet tall, though she was only five feet. She was energetic, bubbly sweet and brassy – all at the same time. The best part was her hair, long with tight curls. It was wild and untamed, and as alive and expressive as her commanding personality, which I have to admit intimidated me at first. I resisted the urge to turn away from her powerful energy. Instead I anchored myself – nervously and took a breath to calm myself and went into her office.

She grabbed my hands and closed her eyes. She saw my family and my son. Okay, so she had skills. Maybe she did know some stuff. Turned out that she picked up on a lot of details that surprised me. Not many gay people have children adopted from another country, and she was right on with the details. I started to relax. A few minutes into the reading she suddenly sat straight up. Her eyes popped open and she said, "You are a medium."

There it was. It is one thing to hear it inside my head from my grandmother – and from my mom (after all, my mom thinks I'm a superstar). But here *she* was. A stranger, a psychic, telling me I was a 'medium.' She became my first and only mentor in 'mediumship.'

She helped me understand that each person is in charge of his or her own power and Spirit wants to help. We practiced how to interpret and understand how it "feels" when a passed loved one is trying to communicate with someone.

I learned that each medium is very different. She was very visual, which is known as Clairvoyance. I am very *feeling*, which is known as Clairsentience. In this journey of discovery, I began to *feel* when a passed loved one was coming through. However, I still could not distinguish who it was and what they wanted to communicate. I had to find a way to figure it out. As my confidence grew, I realized I had been waiting for Spirit to help me figure it out and Spirit had been waiting for me. So, I took charge, I organized everyone like a family portrait. I had everyone stand in a specific spot around the person I was reading. If there was a spirit present, I knew who it was because of the position in the lineup. It became much easier to communicate with each visiting spirit and understand that spirit's relationship with the client. I began using all my "Clair" abilities together, just like we use all of our five senses together.

It wasn't all smooth sailing. Like anything else, psychic abilities work like a muscle. Practice and training are the only ways to hone psychic abilities. Some things I learned the hard way. There were some symbols I misinterpreted before I became clear in the knowledge of my Symbol Dictionary, but with years of study and training and practice I have become accomplished.

IMPORTANCE OF A "SOUL TRIBE"

Since the time I began this journey of transformation I have met a lot of unique people – people with whom I have grown so close so quickly that it amazes me. There is usually an immediate recognition and resonance, as if we have all been waiting for a 'reunion.' Together, we form what I call a soul tribe. A spiritual family. To walk the path of Spirit alone can be daunting. It is a great blessing to be able to share experiences and insights with like-minded soul-siblings, learning from one another with trust and love. The 'tribe' supports each one's spiritual deepening and provides witness and confirmation to transformation.

As you walk your path of discovery and transformation, be open to recognizing your soul-tribe family. It will greatly assist you because with this soul family you are never alone.

My mentor and those in my soul-tribe advised me, first and foremost, to create an on switch and an off switch. It's necessary to be able to turn your abilities on and off. In the beginning everything's neat and fun, because you are just starting to learn, and you aren't yet so very sensitive. I wondered, "Why would anyone want to turn this off? This is great." But now I get it. The longer you do this and the more you practice, the stronger and more sensitive you become.

Imagine trying to sleep during a rock and roll concert. Keeping your abilities on all the time can seem just like that. Spirits wake you up in the middle of the night just because they know you can communicate with them. My on/off switch is a door. When it is open, I am "open for business" and "willing to communicate." My mentor uses a light switch. I have heard of an open/close sign, and a light bulb. You can use many things. This will help you live a regular life.

Another way is to create a written contract, write out on paper that no spirit is to disturb or wake you in your sleep and that your body needs to recharge/rest. It is best to put it in your own verbiage. Sign it and put it on your nightstand. You will find that you get a better night's sleep. You may think this sounds ridiculous. My first thought was, "What does Spirit care about a written piece of paper?" What you are doing is setting an intention. By writing it you are backing it up by putting energy into that intention in the 'real' world, thereby strengthening the intention.

Practicing the on/off switch empowers your subconscious to choose when your abilities are fully awakened and when you can relax. This helps to strengthen the abilities as well, because they get to rest on the "off" time.

The written contract helps your subconscious control when to allow passed loved ones to communicate. Both methods are about intention. Naturally, you can create your own method of the 'on/off switch.' I strongly recommend that you do, because the longer you train in psychic and mediumship abilities, the more sensitive you will become. There will come a time when it becomes harder to create an on/off switch, so do heed the advice of those who have gone before you.

My mentor started me on my path. She helped me focus, gave me wise counsel and assisted my evolution. Initially, her mentoring put me on the fast track. We are, though, different in our abilities. Her Clairvoyant means she receives most of her messages by visual pictures, which I do not. I am an "empath, a Clairsentient-medium" – which means I sense and feel the energy and personality of the passed loved one. This difference between me and my mentor forced me to learn a lot on my own. I set forth on a determined self-discovery. I read a lot of books, and at some point, understood that my greatest revelations come through meditation.

For me, meditation is the easiest way to communicate with my Guides. I made the choice to meditate for hours a day and we created what I call a "Symbol Dictionary." It is my guide to translating the symbols that appear in my readings. It represents what those symbols mean to me. Every person is unique and communicates with Spirit in a unique way, so if you make a Symbol Dictionary of symbols it will be uniquely your own, relevant only to you only because you made it.

In the dictionary some symbols will be similar but have a different meaning. That is where our intuition comes into play. One day I felt I had gone as far as I could go with my symbols and yet felt certain that there were many more. And once again, Spirit stepped in. Like magic, an amazing Metaphysical University called Delphi University appeared on the Internet. Immediately I enrolled in their In-Depth Channeling

Course to become a "certified medium." And I was not disappointed. This Spiritual/Metaphysical University did not teach tricks to connect. The course reminded me of 'who we truly are,' the Divine light within us. We are spiritual beings. And we are connected with each other and are also a part of the Divine.

When the class ended, that understanding became a part of me. My entire being changed and my purpose in life, along with my readings, became clear and full of light.

I truly believe that everything is energy. Energy is matter and non-matter. And Energy is power: the power or strength to move (or work) one force to another. Energy never dies, it just transforms. Energy is made up of light and sound (frequency). Emotions are a frequency. And love is the closest frequency we know to Spirit or Source (God). When I connect to passed loved ones, I connect with love and light. Being an Empath was one of my greatest challenges, but is now my greatest asset, because I use the high vibration (frequency) of love to connect people to the ones who have passed.

Even if a relationship is difficult or does not end on good terms, the frequency of love connects us and heals us. One must know sorrow to know love because we live in a world of duality. And by living in a world of contrasts we learn about Life.

As a psychic/medium I have a different perspective on "death." To speak of death is uncomfortable for most people. The phrase he or she "is in a better place" is often not a comfort for the people left behind – because what they want is the loved one back. In reality, it *is* a better place. If people could see what I see, and feel what I feel, they would be comforted.

When I connect with a loved one, I sense the personality. Say for example, a father who was sometimes too harsh or strict with his children. He was probably raised that way and therefore was not comfortable with showing affection. I get a good sense of this and express it to my clients, so they then know I understand their father very well. I explain what I am feeling in connecting with him. The spirit/soul "has lightened," the father now freer and flowing. He is more willing to be expressive and share his love and emotions. When the family understands why he acted as he did and was not expressive of emotions, a deeper bond is built. It is amazing – and beautiful!

I consider that transition to a new dimension of life like graduating. The life we are living here is meant for our growth, but the spirit world is so much easier. Our loved ones are still with us whenever we want or need them. Just because we can't see them doesn't mean they are not "seeing" us. They are as close as ever. They are without sorrow, without aches and pains. It is those of us who are left behind that are bereft.

Those of us with the gifts of psychic ability and mediumship must lead with understanding and compassion. That is always key.

During this journey of discovery, the support of my family, parents and siblings was incredible. I felt I had entered into crazy land, yet they gave me a non-judgmental ear. It is my hope that you will have such support in your spiritual journey. It's also true though that I have lost friends I considered close and dear. They could not understand and could not accept me. Should you choose this path, you can expect that your soul-tribe will appear and will become your support. I pray you allow it.

As I review my story, I see that's it been an incredible journey. What I thought was a curse became a blessing. I am truly honored to have traveled this road. I would not change anything I have had to go through. Many times, I have been told that it is extremely rare to develop one's psychic abilities so fast. My answer is that I have been a dedicated – almost obsessive – student. We all have psychic abilities and can develop them. You may not want to be a professional psychic. You may just want to listen to your intuition, which is your soul talking. You can be confident that you are hearing your 'higher self.'

Life can be so much easier if we follow our true path by listening to our inner voice. And I want to help. I am writing my story to give you hope. If you don't understand what you are feeling or why, if your sensitivities have brought you to rock bottom and you don't see the light at the end of the tunnel, be assured that I know what that's like – because I've been there.

Though you may feel you are alone, I know you are not alone. Ask for help. Your angels and guides are there for you. Remember that you have to ask. Yes, they have to be asked. Keep asking and wait and watch for the subtle nudge. Assistance and guidance come in many ways, as though on the wind – from a stranger, a friend or family member, even a pet.

The thing to do? Learn to listen. I realize we learn differently. What works for me may not work for you – but I want to share with you what I have learned and what has worked for me. Perhaps it will help you on your Spiritual Journey.

CHAPTER 4

ENERGY, ESSENCE, AND THE LIGHT WITHIN

It took a while for me to feel comfortable with my psychic gift, but I was soon asking Spirit the "tough" questions. Who is God (Source/ Universe)? What is Spirit? What are we? What are we made of? How can I communicate with Spirit (Angels and Guides)? Why do so many psychics get different answers to these questions if we are all speaking to the same Spirit? Where is Heaven (spirit realm/astral plane, Summerland)?

I asked, "What are we?" Spirit answered, "We are energy." That answered my question, but it didn't give me understanding. I realize now that I wasn't specific enough. I have learned that when we ask for something (same is true when we wish and when we pray) we need to be *very* specific. As I asked for understanding, more was revealed. A detail to remember here is that our human mind can only understand situations within our reality.

As our minds expand to handle "more reality," changes do occur in our "vibration" or energy. Then there's the question, 'So, if we are energy, what is God?' Simple. God is the Source. Think of it this way. God is all energy and we are little pieces of energy expressed from the Source. To my mind this explains, "Made in his own image."

THE TRINITY

Let me share with you my concept of the Trinity. God is the source of all things created, and then there is the Son of God. I consider this to be the "Divine Masculine." Everything, and I do mean everything, that is made of matter is the Son of God, such as Earth, Trees, you, me, the universe, sun, men, women, etc. But matter is just matter, it has no life – and that is where The Holy Spirit comes in. In this scenario the Holy Spirit is the "Divine Feminine," bringing life (vital essence/ Prana) to everything. It breathes life into you, me, the plants, trees, water, fruits, etc.

When I first heard of this concept it took me by surprise, but something inside me "knew" it was right for me. I was given a good grasp of what Spirit is. Spirit is all around us and in us. It is Prana, the vital essence of all things, and is why we can connect with each other – because we are all expressions of Spirit. It is an unusual way of explaining the Trinity, but it works for me.

We are energy, and life is about our energy flow. This is why deep breathing is so important. Fresh water and foods that come straight from the ground and aren't modified or chemically treated have more Prana (life energy) to sustain us and make us feel better. The more we process them or chemically treat them, the more they lose vital essence (Prana) and slow our spiritual energy flow.

Now would probably be a good time to explain how or what I see, sense, and feel when I do intuitive readings. When I hold someone's hands I watch and feel the energy flow in the body. I watch for symbols and how the energy flows. Smooth, rough, circular, fast, sporadic, etc. I also look at the light of the soul or spirit of the individual. The *light* tells me about their spirit/soul and lessons they have learned in this and other lifetimes.

The *energy flow* tells me about what is going on now. When I watch the energy flow and see that the energy is blocked or not flowing correctly, I focus on that "strand" of energy and pull it. That strand of energy – its color, shape, how it feels – allows me to see what it may be tied to and why it is not flowing correctly. I think of Spirit (or Holy Spirit) as the flow of energy within the person.

I can also see the light in the person. When the light has a very deep, beautiful, and strong feeling, there is instant connection. When I connect with that light, it is one of the most exciting parts of the reading because it is the purest part of the reading.

PRANA MEDITATION

Allow me to share one meditation exercise to increase Prana. This is an incredible exercise that I recommend be done on a regular basis. It is good for many things. It will help you connect with Spirit, and an ancillary blessing I found for me is that it helps with my little daily aches and pains.

Begin the meditation by closing your eyes and imagining the rhythm of the ocean. Imagine the air around you filled with Prana (vital essence). Picture this vital essence as the color pink, for Love and Spirit have this color. Breathe in as that ocean wave you're imagining goes up, through your solar plexus (just below your rib cage, where your ribs meet in center). Allow the vital essence to go through your nervous system and fill every fiber. Picture it is removing and replacing the toxins in your body.

When the wave peaks, hold the breath just for a second and slowly let it out. Do not force your breath. Your breath should always be natural but extended. Continue to do this for a few minutes. If you breathe in the vital essence on a regular basis you will feel a great difference.

A QUESTION OF HEAVEN AND HELL

My last big question for Spirit was about Heaven (the Astral Plane/Summerland). Where is it? Does it exist? Is it full of clouds? Is it way up high in the universe, etc.? I was told that since we are all just energy and energy never dies, we do not die. We just transform.

We transition to a different frequency (higher vibration) of energy. That leaves the question, where is Heaven? The answer Spirit gave me was, All around us. There are worlds and worlds around us that we don't see. Just because we can't see them does not mean they don't exist. This is easiest to explain as dimensions. We share this planet with other life forms. We don't see them because they exist in a different realm or reality.

Spirit cannot be seen, and we can see only the matter in the world. We live in the world of the Son of God. You are the part of the "Trinity" that is the Son of God. If Spirit is what gives life to all things and is all around us, wouldn't it only make sense that the Spirit world is all around us too?

I have heard of the many stages of Heaven, though I have not been given any information about them from Spirit. I guess it is not my time to know. I trust that I will know when it is time. But I can tell you this: there is NO place called Hell. Some people feel they do not deserve forgiveness or love and thus they are undeserving of "Heaven." They "create" their own personal hell here.

I must stress how important it is to elevate your vibration by emanating Love and extending forgiveness. Respect others as they are. When we respect and honor our differences, we learn the most from each other. And when we evolve spiritually, we will experience the Unity of the One Source.

DIFFERENT STORIES – SAME MESSAGE

My story may not align with yours. Though your story is different, the underlying messages will be so similar you will likely be shocked. That is an amazing thing about Spirit. Remember the question, "Why do so many psychics get different answers to questions if we are all speaking to the same Spirit?" Look closely and I think you will find that it's the story that's different. The message is usually the same.

You may be religious, I do not consider myself religious. I consider myself spiritual. I use the term God, Source or Universe interchangeably – because to me it is all the same and I use it with honor and respect. Before I do readings, before any of my events, I always start with an opening prayer that starts like this: "I honor and acknowledge the forces of Light…" That covers it! In my personal opinion I don't think God would mind if you called him Bob, if you meant it with honor and respect.

Spirit is always here trying to help and communicate with us. We just need to slow down and listen with all of our Being. God is always with us because God is within us. We are the Light, we are God-expressing.

CHAPTER 5

ANGELS AND GUIDES

L ET'S TALK ABOUT MEDITATION. I have many angels and guides, and I contact them through meditation. (I do, though, know some people who reach their angels and guides through other means.) Angels have never had a body, but they usually show themselves as either male or female. The first angels that helped me with my healing were Jophiel and Raphiel. My teacher angel is Metatron. I have a deep fondness for Sandolphin. Through the years my guides have changed. The first one's name was David. And there have been others: Tiger Lily, Zy, Qak – just to name a few.

Through the ages a great deal has been said about meditation, but in this age I ask you to rethink the old concepts. You do not have to sit lotus style and/or chant for hours. My personal preference is to sit in a quiet dark room. The meditation can take minutes or hours. You have many options – for example, meditating while taking a bath. Any time you clear your mind and focus on being present to the moment you are meditating – and the more meditation you do, the more you will experience a sense of calm.

The best advice I can give you about meditation is to start in short increments of 5 to 15 minutes and build from there. Guided meditation CDs have worked well for me. There are also CDs that induce self-hypnosis. They are similar to guided meditations but seem to put you into a deeper meditative state. There are also CDs to help you unlock your psychic abilities. Most likely some will work for you and others will not.

On my journey I found that I was guided via meditation and the power of intention. It is my hope that you will also sit in the stillness – and *open your self* to the whispers of your angels and guides.

ANGELS

My angels. They came first. The important point to remember is this: everything is energy, and angels are the lightest energy. Angels vibrate at an extremely high vibration. I explained earlier that they first appeared to me as simple colors. Initially, I imagined myself surrounded by colors, chakra colors (more on chakras later). I don't know exactly when the colors changed into angels. One day I simply noticed that I didn't have to imagine the colors anymore, nor did I have to picture the angels going around my body. I didn't have to picture them healing – they just did it, moved through me without my asking or willing. Have you ever seen the natural flow of a stream? How it gracefully swirls, dips and twists? Imagine that as air and color, and beauty and wonder vibrating.

As the colors danced around me that day, it seemed as if the angels were singing and I could almost hear them thinking. Very enjoyable, it was – so I began looking forward to meditation not just for the healing but also for the joy of watching and listening to the beautiful light show. And after every meditation I felt refreshed and renewed.

There are many books about angels. Doreen Virtue, for whom I have the greatest respect, writes many. My mother is a huge fan of hers and purchased many of Doreen's books for me, but I found that I was able to read only some portion of them. Though I truly enjoyed them, I found

I couldn't get very far in reading them because Spirit always stopped me. Distracted me.

You might think this odd, but it is common. After many times of trying, I caught on to the pattern and closed my eyes and called my guides and asked, "Why is it I get distracted?"

The response was simple. Angels appear to each of us differently. If our mind needs them to have wings with feathers, that is how they appear. Doreen serves as a channel for the angels to speak to many people—people who do not feel that they can speak directly or trust their own communication. Angels can communicate with us directly – through emotions, symbols, colors and thought. If you are curious or have questions, just ask. They may provide you a different answer, one that pertains just to you.

I have felt the presence of other people's angels though I've never seen or spoken with them. Their angels sometimes communicate through my angels and guides, and because my angels understand and feel comfortable with their 'symbolic dictionary' the reading is easier and less confusing. Everyone's symbolic dictionary is personal and because it's personal it is by definition different. Other people's angels show themselves to me as colors and feelings. I will not say much more about angels except that they are beautiful, incredible, lovely creatures – and full of love and compassion. It took me a long time to get used to being in the presence of angels because I was overwhelmed with emotions. I do feel blessed now, for I have developed an openness sufficient to communicate with them.

GUIDES

You might be wondering what the difference is between Angels and Guides. The way it was explained to me (through my guidance) is that guides have lived some sort of life. They usually prefer to choose a form and a sex. Angels, though, have never been born to earth so they've never had a physical body. Guides have traveled through many lifetimes and learned many lessons. You can consider them enlightened beings – and yes, I'm talking reincarnation. Rather than moving on to transcendence, they choose to stay here to assist and 'guide' us on our journey to transcendence. The vibration of the Guides is not as high or fast as the vibration of Angels.

You may wonder why we need both. The answer is, their different perspectives on how best to assist us are unique. An angel sees things in the highest perspective, closest to God, but angels do not quite understand the human aspects, for example jobs, food, paying bills, etc. Angels are not concerned with those things for they have had no experience with them. Guides have lived, so they understand that we have to live, but they also want us to grow spiritually. When we have both angels and guides working with us, we can be sure we've got a good team.

EARTH ANGELS

I've recently heard a lot about earth angels. At first, this had me very confused. I didn't understand. The explanation given to me was that angels have never been born, so how could there be earth angels? Spirit explained it to me this way: "We are all energy. When our body dies our souls are then free to lift up and become lighter energy again. How we choose to live this life determines how light our energy will be. The lighter the energy, the faster it will vibrate. The faster it vibrates, the closer it will be to God. The closest vibrating energy to God is angel energy. Thus, one can become an angel from earth if one lives life well. Strive to be an earth angel. Spread your energetic wings." At a personal level, that's what I'm shooting for. Our vibration is our personal energy frequency. The lower frequency energies relate to anxiety, fear, depression, sadness, etc. With a higher frequency, life flows more in synchronicity, peace, calm, etc.

THE APPEARANCE OF MY GUIDES

Let's talk about my guides. My first two were animals. I didn't understand at first what the purpose was of an animal guide. I am still not sure I fully understand, but I do know it's important to keep an open mind. My first animal guide was a butterfly and it disappointed me. I was a 40-year-old man and a bluish-purple butterfly showed up. What was I supposed to do with that? I felt blocked and tried hard to advance. Actually, I tried too hard. I have learned since that if you try too hard you can stop yourself from naturally letting things happen. (We will get to that subject later.) I didn't see or hear anything, literally got nothing – except a butterfly. Not very powerful, I thought. If I had to have an animal, I wanted a wolf or a tiger – but I had no choice. I didn't choose the blue-purple butterfly, but I did have to accept it – because trying to convince this butterfly in my mind's eye to shift into something awesome, like a wizard or an Indian chief, was not working.

During my meditations, day after day I watched this butterfly flap around. For months, that is all it did. I asked my shamanic friend in my soul tribe, "What is the purpose of this butterfly?" She politely pointed out two important things. First, a butterfly is a symbol of transformation. You are getting ready to blossom into something beautiful when you are ready to accept this guide. My friend's second point was that your third eye isn't as blocked as you think if you can see the butterfly.

I walked away feeling better about my third eye and when the butterfly showed up again, I simply said okay and accepted it as my guide. The butterfly landed on my forehead (where the third eye is) and I felt a slight tingle. I honestly think I got a butterfly kiss. For about a week that continued, until one day the butterfly landed on my forehead and melted into my third eye. He remains there, still. I think in a way we have merged. Ironically, I sometimes miss the blue-purple wings, but I still feel the butterfly.

This leads to a question that most spiritual teachers debate: Are guides an aspect (part of us)? Or are they spiritual beings that are external beings? The correct answer is really not known. We all have our own opinion. I personally think they can be both.

My next guide was a simple brown-black barn owl and I liked him. He was an obvious match for me at the time as I had hit the metaphysical books and classes fast and hard. Neither of these animals talked. Their image would simply pop into my head. Sometimes, as I studied, I found it difficult to absorb what I had just learned. I was reading too much too fast, and at that point the owl would pop into my head, letting me know to slow down and let it soak in. I thanked him for reminding me.

The more I recognized him, the more I took his advice and listened, the more he started showing up in other parts. He began showing up in my personal life. Many times when I wanted to say something, he would pop up and I'd know it wasn't the right time to say what I had in mind. I knew we had become a team when I was catching myself before he could pop up. One day he showed up – but he had changed from a brown-black owl to a white owl. He looked proud and it was as if we, as a team, had graduated. Now I have a white owl guide, for he is still a guide, but I only see him on occasion.

Recently, another animal guide appeared. A raven. Though I've never been keen on ravens or crows and find them kind of scary-looking, I was interested in what the raven had to teach me. What I learned is that the raven shows up when I have a difficult time ahead. As an Empath, I do not like confrontation. I try to be the "peacemaker." I don't like the way the energy of conflict feels and looks. Raven has taught me that I am not the one who needs to fix things and that things happen because they must – because the outcome is supposed to happen. She is here to let me know that I must challenge myself to stay true to myself and allow the energy to simply flow. She is my toughest messenger and is many layered. We are still at the beginning of our relationship.

YOUR FIRST GUIDE

Let's talk about your first guide – the one you seem to create a special bond with, the one you never forget. Every guide and angel is special, but your first guide is extra special. Some people refer to it as the gatekeeper, or key holder. Yes, this bond is usually the strongest, and that is why it introduces itself first. Though your guides are always with you, they choose when to introduce themselves. The gatekeeper is extra important because he or she decides who or what spirit can or can't interact with you.

Remember that the spirit world is all around us. It is at a higher vibration, which means we can't see it. The gatekeeper is like your personal assistant for the spirit world – screening your calls, emails, and bad spirits. The gatekeeper screens any energy that might mess with your mojo. It aims to keep you on track.

I was ready to meet my first guide. I was in a meditation I created. (At the end of this chapter I will go through a meditation to help you contact your guide.) I told my guide I was ready to meet him, to please come forth. And I waited and waited. A couple days later, during another meditation, a tall man in a green robe comes walking toward me. It's a simple green pullover robe that covers his entire body and hangs all the way to his calves. He wears simple sandals and as he walks closer I see that he is tall – well over six feet, and his hair dark brown with big loose curls. He's a handsome man with a genuinely kind face and pink cheeks, and a smile that would make you picture Santa Claus. I wondered if it was Santa. Great, I thought, my spirit guide is Santa…but it wasn't Santa. He was young. And skinny. I stared, but he didn't seem to mind. Suddenly I couldn't help myself – I just hugged him. It felt like home and he hugged me back in a kind way. After the long embrace, I really didn't know what to do. I asked him his name. He just smiled at me and after about five minutes he faded away.

I had nothing I could compare the experience to, so I thought it went well. In meditations, I started calling him frequently, and for a long time when he would appear I would ask his name. This went on for months. He would just politely smile and eventually did tell me his name was David. I have to be honest, I was a little disappointed. I thought his name would be something ancient and powerful. When I told my mother this she quickly rebutted, "David means beloved one." Well, that made me feel better. And now I understand that it is we humans who put names on the guides. To them, names are not important.

When I created my "place of power" David was always there without me having to call him. A place of power is usually a scene or place where you are relaxed and comfortable. My place of power is a lavender field with a large tree in the center of the field. I later found out that he was always there because he is my protector guide, my guardian. He no longer shows his face, but I feel his presence.

Guides are with you from the beginning, from the signing of your soul contract to when you cross back over to the spirit world. Every day I am comforted by his presence, and I thank him for always keeping me out of trouble. When I look back on all the crazy things I did and the fact that I survived, I have him to thank. Thank you, David! I owe you for my safety!

ANOTHER GUIDE

This next one is fun! She just popped in one day. She has long black hair and energy to burn. She smiles all of the time. If you knew me personally you would know it's this guide that influences me the most. Her name is Tiger Lily. I knew her name right away because I had seen a picture of Disney's Peter Pan cartoon character. I asked her if that was her name. She smiled and nodded. She doesn't look like the Disney cartoon but it was a good image to reference. She is young, a teen – and looks Native-American. She is what most would consider a joy guide. She loves Mother Nature and the beauty and wonder of the world – and can see the miracle in everyday life. She loves flowers, herbs, and the scents of Lavender, Basil, Rosemary, Lemons, Tulips and Mint.

She is your typical teenager, silly and funny. She can be a little sarcastic, but in a fun way. She always looks on the bright side and has a great sense of humor. I have to say, I am one of those people who look for the brighter side in everything and she helps me do it. She loves animals, and especially loves butterflies, so as you might guess she was the one responsible for the blue-purple butterfly spirit guide coming to me. She thought it would be funny for me to have a butterfly. She also teaches me to grow and think outside the box, and loves it when I act goofy. I honor her with my laughs – and a positive outlook!

There are many more guides. Some are healer guides, some teacher guides. I sometimes think my owl is part of my teacher guide. I have not met these other guides in person, though I know I use them because I can sense them.

ASCENDED MASTER GUIDE

There's a guide that carries a higher vibration and is more advanced: an Ascended Master guide. An Ascended Master guide is very difficult to contact. Some people meet theirs immediately and for others it takes years. I would not recommend trying to contact an Ascended Master. They come to you – you do not go to them.

An Ascended Master is typically a very wise soul that is well known in history. For example, Jesus, Buddha, Mary Magdalene, Mother Mary, Kwan Yin, Ganesh, etc.

I have just recently met mine and she is Mother Mary. I am extremely honored. As a gay man, raised in the Roman Catholic Church, it was a long road to self-acceptance and to fully embrace who I was, and also to understand that my Maker created me as I am. When Mother Mary came to me as my Ascended Master Guide, I rejoiced. She is the mother of the angels, and I know I am loved.

It took me a long time to get to know one of my Ascended Masters. My mother met hers when she was sixteen – before she met any of her other guides. We are all different, and once again I remind you that Ascended Masters come to you.

UNUSUAL GUIDES

Everything is energy and guides come in many forms. I have met people who have guides in the forms of trees, flowers, rocks, etc. I once received a guide from a meditation/channeling, an unusual and unique experience. All I can say is that he was not of this world. Now he stands behind me in my readings. He is huge and feels like the size of a wall. He is a kind spirit, but he is a being from another planet. He has only come forward in one of my readings, and that was to talk to a person who in this life is human but in past lives was not.

The more we are open-minded, willing to put no limitations on who we think a guide should look or act like, the more angels and guides and other enlightened beings will come to us. I know I will have the honor of working with more. I realize in this journey that anything is possible. The more I open up to endless possibilities, the more incredible things will happen. Guides are just the beginning.

MEDITATION TO MEET YOUR GUIDE

I recommend that you make a recording of you reading this section. (Unless you can memorize it.) This meditation will allow you to relax and be fully in the meditative state. Begin by setting the intention that you are ready to meet your guide. It may take a couple times, so do not get frustrated. That would only delay things. It will happen when it is meant to happen. Here's the technique:

Take a deep, long breath, filling your belly. Hold for a couple seconds, then SLOWLY release the breath. Repeat this two more times and afterward, bring your breath back to normal, but stay focused on your breath. Pay attention to how the breath goes in and slightly pauses, and then out. Allow the breathing to become a pattern, let it relax you. With every breath, your mind and body becomes more relaxed. Follow the breath, until you feel as if you are in a "daydream" state. This is the meditation state.

Once you have achieved that state, imagine a beautiful garden. What would your garden look like? Do you see flowers, trees? Imagine looking up at the beautiful sky. Connect with your garden. What does your garden feel like? Peace, calm, serenity? Try to use all your senses. Imagine the smell of the garden.

Look forward and a path appears. Now what does the path look like? Is it dirt? Or stone? Imagine what it would look like. Take a nice deep breath and allow yourself to become more relaxed. Walk along the path, looking at all the beauty and wonder of the garden.

Find a nice place to sit. As you are sitting there, enjoying your beautiful time in the garden, something in the distance catches your eye. A light. It is a beautiful bright light. As you are looking at the light, notice a silhouette walking toward you emerging from the light. As the silhouette comes toward you, sense knowing this being, sense the love radiating from this being. The being sits next to you. What do you see? What do you feel? You may ask this being anything you wish or you may just want to sit quietly. Once you feel complete, thank the being for introducing itself. Get up and walk back along the path. Every step along the path brings you back to the here-and-now, until you are fully aware of your surroundings.

I strongly suggest that you journal all that you saw and felt, and everything in the garden and everything about the being. That being is your Guide, and you have a relationship with it just like any other relationship. The more you invest in the relationship, the stronger the bond. It is up to you whether you want a strong relationship or not.

CHAPTER 6

HEALING WITH ENERGY AS A MEDIUM

I WAS DRAWN TO HEALING because of my own physical and emotional pain. When I first began my search into metaphysics, I knew something was calling to me, so I tried just about everything available at the time. In my area of the country, southeastern USA, the thing most available was an energy-healing modality called Reiki. There are three levels in Reiki, the third being the Master level. I am not a Master Reiki healer and do not presume to know all about that modality.

My first class was enjoyable, I liked my teacher; she was bubbly and explained everything well, but when it came time to practice on other students and on the teacher, I did not feel "connected." I received high praises from everyone. They said they felt the energy. But I have to be honest: I felt as if I was playing "pretend energy doctor." So I decided Reiki was not for me. I put it on a shelf labeled, "Tried It – Not For Me" – and moved on to other forms.

Then I met Summer. For a long time I shied away from her. She was a gentle, kind, soft-spoken person, but I was just "awakening," so meeting someone with whom I had a true soul connection – a past life connection

—was intimidating. I said to myself, *Am I crazy? What is going on? How do I know her? This is weird!*

So I just avoided connecting with her. Then one day when a group of us got together, I learned she was a Reiki Master. When I told her about the class I had taken, she listened and intuitively picked up that I was now working with different kinds of energy. She suggested that it might be time to try again, and explained that since everything is energy it would help me to understand and feel different forms of energy. I thought about it and concluded it couldn't hurt.

I decided to start all over again and take the same class, but this time I took Summer's class and she emphasized different parts of Reiki, such as the symbols and why they are important, and how to channel the energy and the attunement. The **Reiki attunement** is a powerful spiritual experience. The **attunement** energies are channeled into the student through the **Reiki Master**. The process is guided by the Rei or God-consciousness. And in the process adjustments are made, depending on the needs of the student.

Summer has a lot of Shaman in her, so when she did her attunement, I felt the power of nature and the significance of the plants and animals. To be honest, I was amazed that this sweet, kind, soft-spoken and humble woman had such extreme power. (Never underestimate the quiet, humble ones – they're the ones that don't need to boast.)

And then it came time to practice on her and another student. This time, I could definitely feel the energy come through. It felt like white, warm light coming into my head and out of my hands, so I could send it into the person's body for healing. It was amazing! I intuitively knew where my 'healing' hands needed to go and when to move to the next spot, and even why they needed to move – and knew when I was done. It felt good, felt natural. And I knew I was officially an Energy Healer.

I decided to continue on and take Reiki 2. The big difference in level 2 is that it teaches you how to send healing energy long distance. You can do this in many ways and one way is through using symbols. We all have access to the same universal field, the field of consciousness and knowledge, and can draw from it. Reiki healing symbols serve as one kind of tool for tapping the universal field with intention to access energy for healing and balancing. We use the symbols to connect with different aspects of Reiki. There are five symbols in Reiki Healing. Traditionally, three of the symbols are taught to Reiki 2 students, while the fourth and fifth symbols are reserved to Reiki Master students.

You might wonder how you can send healing long distance? It is simple. Distance and time do not exist in energy. It's like talking on the phone. You talk and instantly the other person can hear it. Sending Reiki symbols for healing energy is like that.

People often ask me how I do readings over the phone or on my radio show. The experience is the same, like that phone conversation. It feels like the person is right next to me. I focus on the person's energy and we are connected.

I never went further with Reiki. The next step in Reiki was to get my Reiki Master's Certification, which would allow me to teach Reiki to other people, but I had noticed that when I was using Reiki my mediumship channels began opening and the traditional Reiki energy started to change. I have huge respect for Reiki, so I felt it would be disrespectful to the Reiki tradition to go for that Mastery—because I couldn't use it in the traditional way. Those who truly honor and love Reiki will understand. It is not about a certificate. It's about honor. I would not dishonor Reiki.

HEALING THROUGH MEDIUMSHIP

I knew I was meant to be a healer when I connected strongly with my mediumship ability. My readings are not what one would consider traditional healing, yet they are a strong form of healing. To be able to connect souls seeking one another, one in this world and one in the spirit world, is a beautiful and healing experience. Deep healing occurs through the connection of the souls. For those participating in my readings, feelings are shared and things not said in life here can be said, so healing can occur. For me it is the privilege of the opportunity to heal those participating in my readings. I can help heal their relationship, and I am most grateful that I can be a part of this healing.

Intuitive readings and intuitive counseling are other forms of healing. I can connect a client with angels and spirit guides, and this helps the individual connect with the higher self. I have found that when people feel stuck in their life and do not know why, it is usually because they are not listening to their spiritual self. I can help them connect to the heart-self. Life is a lot simpler if we just listen to our hearts. That is where our soul lives, and though we will always experience some rocky times, we are meant to learn from the journey. This is how we grow spiritually.

DIFFERENT STYLES

There are different styles and different types of energy healings. Each healer's mind works differently so the way the healing is expressed is unique to that healer. I explained earlier about psychic abilities. The same concept applies for the healer. The most effective healing is accomplished when the healer is connected to his or her inner core, the essential self.

Allow me to use my Reiki master as an example. Summer has the heart of a Shaman and has studied Shamanism. She connects with nature in every aspect: plants, animals, sky, etc. Though she teaches traditional Reiki she also practices other healing modalities. In her healing practice, the Shamanic energy and earth magic is clearly experienced. My point is this: if you choose to follow the path of energy healing, allow yourself to feel your true inner influence, and then use your imagination and go with it.

For me, my expression of healing is in cooperation with the angels. Their presence infuses a large influence in my energy healings. When I do my healings, my angels are front and center, and my clients are also aware of them. The expansion of energy in the room is electric.

I spread my energetic wings, say my opening healing prayer – and begin. I sense the colors that need to be called forth for specific healing purposes, though most of the time it is the pure golden-white healing light that I use to fill the client's light body (the etheric body) to begin the healing. A lot of healers get information and visions, but I do not, although I have received information on occasion. I intuitively know where to move my hands and when the energy slows and stops.

My primary focus is on the chakras. The chakra system is believed to be where energy is gathered and distributed throughout our body to keep the body's energy flowing smoothly. Each chakra represents a physical, mental and spiritual body. There are seven main chakras, positioned along the spine. Chakra means "wheel," and each of the seven chakras are represented by a specific color.

THE CHAKRA SYSTEM

The word "chakra" has its roots in the Sanskrit language, coming from the Hindus thousands of years ago. What are chakras? There are many definitions but they're basically the same, so I will give you mine. Chakras are energy points in and out of your subtle body that helps the flow of energy. We are going to review the seven basic/main chakras – or energy points – along the spine and in the head. We will start from the bottom of the spine and work up. The chakras are not physical. They're part of the "subtle body."

At the top of your head is the Crown Chakra. It faces upward, like a cone sitting on top. At the base of the spine is the Root Chakra. It faces down toward the ground. The rest of the seven chakras have a front and back – and you pull energy in front and back. Though they are described as wheels, they are shaped like a cone. Their purpose is to aid the healing of your spiritual and physical body.

The chakras link our spirit (or soul) to the spiritual world. I think of them as a "cord" that attaches soul and body. Each chakra has a symbolic color.

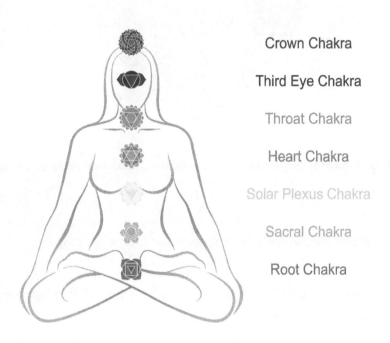

Crown Chakra

Third Eye Chakra

Throat Chakra

Heart Chakra

Solar Plexus Chakra

Sacral Chakra

Root Chakra

ROOT CHAKRA

Root Chakra: Represents our foundation and our feelings of being grounded.

Location: Base of spine in tailbone area (adrenal glands).

Emotional issues: Survival issues, such as financial independence, money and food, as well as basic trust.

The root chakra relates to stability, survival, primal energy, fear, anxiety, and structure.

Mantra: I AM / LAM

SACRAL CHAKRA

Sacral Chakra: Our connection, and ability to accept others and accept new experiences.

Location: Lower abdomen, about two inches below the navel and two inches in (gonads, kidneys).

Emotional issues: Sense of abundance, wellbeing, pleasure and sexuality. It's about intimacy, creativity, sexuality, emotions, expression of needs, giving-receiving, desires, and letting go.

Mantra: I feel /VAM

SOLAR PLEXUS

Solar Plexus Chakra: Our confidence and ability to be in control of our lives.

Location: Upper abdomen in the stomach area (pancreas).

Emotional issues: Self-worth, self-confidence and self-esteem. If over-stimulated, may get power-hungry or controlling.

It is about wisdom and power, willpower, personal authority, purpose, self-control, and gut instinct.

Mantra: I do/ RAM

HEART CHAKRA

Heart Chakra: Our ability to love.

Location: Center of chest just above the heart (thymus).

Emotional issues: Love, joy, inner peace.

It is about love, healing, compassion, God, sharing, relating, emotional balance, connection, hope, and respect for self and others.

Mantra: I Love/ YUM

THROAT CHAKRA

Throat Chakra: Our ability to communicate.

Location: Throat (Thyroid).

Emotional issues: Communication, and self-expression of our feelings and the truth.

It is about creativity, communication, seeing the whole individual, speech, articulation, openness, yin-yang, and truth.

Mantra: I speak/ HUM

THIRD EYE CHAKRA

Third Eye Chakra: Our ability to focus on and see the big picture.

Location: Forehead, between the eyes - also called the Brow Chakra (pituitary).

Emotional issues: Intuition, imagination, wisdom. And the ability to think and make decisions.

It is about insight or understanding beyond our five senses. Also, being of service.

Mantra: I see/ SHAM

CROWN CHAKRA

Crown Chakra: The highest chakra represents our ability to be fully connected spiritually.

Location: The very top of the head (pineal).

Emotional issues: Inner and outer beauty. Our connection to spirituality and pure bliss.

It is about spiritual understanding, cosmic connection, wisdom, spiritual connection, enlightenment, and knowing.

Mantra: I understand/ OM

HUMAN ENERGY SYSTEM

Our body is made up of Divine Masculine Energy and Divine Feminine Energy. Seek to balance these energies. When they're not balanced, we tend to look for life partners to balance us, but seldom does that work well. Rarely do we achieve complete balance, so it's best to just be aware of these energies.

Divine Feminine Energy: Intuition, nurturing, healing, calm, emotional awareness, plus expression and communication of emotions.

Divine Masculine Energy: Logic, reason, energy of action, firmness, survival, common sense, and ease of acquiring material needs.

The left side of our body is made up of Divine Feminine Energy. The right side is made up of Divine Masculine Energy.

Chakra	ROOT CHAKRA- "THE PRESENCE"	SACRAL CHAKRA- "THE EMOTIONAL ONE"	SOLAR PLEXUS "THE ACHIEVER"	HEART CHAKRA "THE ONE WHO CARES"	THROAT CHAKRA "THE EXPRESSER"	THIRD EYE CHAKRA- "THE VISIONARY"	CROWN CHAKRA "THE ANGELIC ONE"
Color	Red	Orange	Yellow	Green	Light blue	Indigo	Violet (or white)
Location	Base of the spine	Inches below the navel	Between lower rows of ribs	Center of chest above the heart	Throat	Forehead -between the eyes	Very top of the head
Functions: Purpose	Security, safety	Emotions, feelings	Will, personal power	Love for oneself and others	Expression, communication	Vision, intuition	Awareness, consciousness connection
Organ/System	Adrenal glands	Gonads, Kidneys	Pancreas	Thymus	Thyroid	Pituitary	Pineal
Balanced	Stability, vibrancy, health	Happiness, joy, sensuality, creativity	Strength, courage, willpower	Peace, acceptance, easy gives/receives love	Smooth communications	Intuition, creativity, dream recall, visualization	Peace, wisdom
Overactive	Sluggish, constipated	Obsessive attachments, oversensitive	Controlling, competitive power-hungry	Co-dependency, jealousy, lack of empathy	Gossip, criticism, excessive/ loud talking, hyperthyroidism	Headaches, nightmares, lack of focus	Daydreaming, feel superior to others
Underactive	Fear, anxiety, diarrhea	Obsessive attachments, oversensitive	Powerlessness, chronic fatigue, poor digestion	Shyness, loneness, bitterness	Inability to express one-self, quiet speaking, hypothyroidism	Inability to imagine or visualize	Skepticism, difficulty thinking
Crystals	Red jasper, smoky quartz, hematite	Carnelian, orange aventurine	Citrine, tiger eye, honey calcite	Rose quartz, green aventurine	Lapis lazuli, blue lace agate, sodalite	Amethyst	Clear quartz
Mantra	I am/ LAM	I feel /VAM	I do /RAM	I Love /YUM	I Speak/HUM	I See/SHAM	I Understand/ OM

TOOLS FOR HEALING

Many healers use tools to assist them in healing. Common tools are drums, rattles, chimes, etc. – to break the vibration of the negative energy. Other common tools are oils, incense, and other aromatherapies. Healing and Oracle Cards can be used before the therapy takes place, in order to give the healer an idea of where to start. Crystals, wands and pendulums are also used. I use soft music, a lavender pillow for the eyes, and chimes and a feather to smooth the aura field.

For group healings, sound is often used. This is achieved with sound bowls and/or other instruments played to the same frequency (or vibration) as your chakras – to clear the energy.

Every healing session is different, because every client is different. Let me share what happens when I do an energy session. I always start by opening up to Spirit, with a moment of silence, a quiet meditation and prayer for healing, and for protection of the highest good and light, love and healing.

When I sense and feel the pure white light of Source come upon me, I know I am ready to begin. At this point I feel the warmth of the white light, and also feel electricity coursing throughout my body. (This experience seems to be unique to me, for I am told it is not common, so please don't expect it of yourself.)

I start at the feet and spend a few seconds there so I know they are "open." If anything needs to be flushed out or removed from the body, it now has an exit point. I then start at the crown chakra and begin the connection, and usually spend a while there. I may start getting images, impressions or feelings. I have talked to many healers who have told me incredible stories and incredible images they have seen. Since I have shared this in an earlier chapter, I won't repeat it here.

As the client's "light body" fills with healing light and gets lighter and fluffier, its sense of joy becomes very apparent. Then I let my intuition, guides, angels and other healers guide me to where I need to move my hands to send energy where it needs to go. Energy is an incredible thing. I can expand it in areas that need to be cleared and with more healing light I can break up the vibration of negative energy. Energy may also be expanded around hurt or sore muscles to relax the tension and diminish pain.

I have had many energy healings. I think it is important to have your energy cleared and cleaned. I clean my energy field all the time. You may not realize what may be caught up in your own energy field, such as judgments, resentments, pain, hurtful memories, and other kinds of negative energy. And, it is easier to 'read' my client's energy when mine is clear. Thus, because of the work I do, I get an energy clearing on a regular basis. I enjoy them. They make me feel great and keep me clean and clear.

Every healer is unique. You should know your healer and trust the healer because the healer is "clearing" you. If this individual is not "clear" then he or she should not be doing work on you. When I use the word "clear" (and this is just my opinion) I mean that the energy should feel good to you. The energy should not make you feel as though you're in turmoil. You wouldn't submit to surgery with an unlicensed doctor, so why trust your energy to an individual that can't handle his or her own energy?

Alcohol and drugs affect energy so this factor should be kept in mind when deciding on an energy healer. The healer should not have had any alcohol for at least 24 hours before doing a healing – and in my opinion, this goes for any psychic work.

A healing from a medium may be different than a healing from another kind of healer. A medium works with many frequencies at a time. Energy is light and sound. Light and sound are color and frequency. Mediums heal with light and love – and have no encumbrance from the law of time and space. We can hold many frequencies at a time. This means we can call upon light beings from other dimensions to help us, including angels, past loved ones, past surgeons, and other light beings from many dimensions. It can make the experience a lot more intense and heal all three of your bodies (physical, spiritual and mental/emotional).

During your energy healing with a medium you might have memories of past loved ones come up – and some may be beautiful and some may not. The memories are coming up because the medium is connecting with past loved ones and they are helping you heal through memories. It is a beautiful connection, so enjoy and embrace the love.

Other people who have passed over may come through. Sometimes during energy healings I "work" with doctors or surgeons that have passed. They come through to help this person heal old wounds or get them ready for the next step. Most people call this Psychic Surgery. I can feel the beautiful light-beings that come to help and am grateful for their assistance. I have seen and heard many of my clients rave about subsequent progress.

We all have psychic abilities. Some individuals strongly feel their psychic abilities, others work to develop them, and some suppress them. Remember that you have the light within you and that light – the soul – is the direct connection with Source. You are limitless – but you must be willing to take the leap of faith. It's never too late to change your life if you give it the effort it deserves and if you believe in (and within) yourself.

CHAPTER 7

DEVELOPING YOUR PSYCHIC ABILITIES

EVERYTHING I TEACH IN my psychic development classes is taught through experience. What I teach is what I have learned via communication with Spirit and through a combination of research from Internet, books, courses, seminars, and Delphi University. Yes, I have done extensive research in psychic development, so what I teach is what I have learned and I'm here to encourage you to find the message from Spirit – that pertains to you!

Before we even talk about psychic abilities we need to know who (or what) we are. Pierre Teilhard de Chardin said, "We are not human beings having a spiritual experience; we are spiritual beings having a human experience."

Notice that I have not said I am going to teach you psychic abilities, because I am not. You already have them. I believe we are born with them and everyone has them.

I found two definitions of psychic on Google:

psy·chic - sī'kik (adjective):

1. Relating to or denoting faculties or phenomena that are apparently inexplicable by natural laws, especially involving telepathy or clairvoyance.

2. "psychic powers"

Synonyms: supernatural, paranormal, otherworldly, supernormal, preternatural, metaphysical, extrasensory, magic, magical, mystical, mystic, occult … more.

Of or relating to the soul or mind. "He dulled his psychic pain with gin."

Synonyms: emotional, spiritual, inner (… and more)

We are all familiar with the first definition. It is the common one, referring to psychic "abilities." The second definition is what I would like to discuss, the definition of the Soul.

We all have the light (soul/spirit) within us. We are born with this light, and it is a light that is psychic before it is human. We connect in the womb. With this light we connect with others without using our human eyes, ears, mouth, etc. We connect psychically. We connect and bond with 'the mother we chose' through our feelings. This is a psychic ability called clairsentience.

Clairsentience is the ability to feel things on a psychic level. You still use it today. For example, when you meet someone new, you may get a good feeling instantly or you may feel there is something "not right." That is your psychic ability – and there is nothing mystical or "evil" about it. It is a spiritual connection. You are connecting with your inner light. This is your natural ability. The more we learn to trust and enhance this ability – the more we practice with it – the brighter it shines. Intuition grows the same way a muscle does, so practice, practice, and practice.

In the book, *The Psychic Being, Soul: Its Nature, Mission and Evolution*, this passage explains it best, "The soul and the psychic being are not exactly the same thing, although their essence is the same. The soul is the Divine spark that dwells at the centre of each being; it is identical with its Divine

Origin; it is the Divine in man. The psychic being is formed progressively around this centre, the soul, in the course of its innumerable lives in the terrestrial evolution, until the time comes when the psychic being, fully formed and wholly awakened, becomes the conscious sheath of the soul around which it is formed. And thus identified with the Divine, it becomes His perfect instrument in the world."

(MOTHER, 1989).

I am not here to teach you psychic abilities. I am here to remind you of what you have forgotten. You were born with these abilities. When you understand that these abilities are natural, you begin to relax and let your abilities shine. When working with these abilities keep in mind that there is no wrong! We are unique individuals, so we "process" information through our Clairs differently.

Flow… we are energy. Energy never stops, so relax and let it move. It is a fluid motion. We often block or hinder the flow within us by trying too hard. If you feel pressure building up anywhere in your body, that is blocked energy. Relax and let it flow naturally.

Honor what you feel and see. At times, a student may worry that what is being seen or felt is somehow wrong, but it is never wrong. Remember, Spirit works in symbols, and what you may be seeing can help build your Symbol dictionary. No matter how silly it may seem, honor what you see.

For example, as I was teaching a class I had students read photos of loved ones. One of the students had a photo of an elderly woman. In her mind's eye she saw a goldfish cracker and thought it silly. I had stressed the importance of writing everything down, so when her time came for sharing, she was hesitant and did not want to say what she saw. Finally she did and the woman whose photo it was had no idea what it meant. The lady who did the reading was embarrassed until we went within and asked, "What does a goldfish cracker mean?"

It wasn't the goldfish cracker that was important – it was the fish symbol. Some religions use 'fish' as a symbol, and the woman in the photo was extremely religious. So the reader soon understood why she visualized a goldfish cracker. Each individual owns a personal set of symbols, and therefore we consult a Spirit Symbol Dictionary.

THE CLAIRS

Clair means "clear sensitivity." Just as our human body has five senses, the psychic part of our being has six clairs. We can translate or interpret what the body senses if we translate what we sense psychically and intuitively. Here's a list of the six clairs.

Clairvoyance means clear seeing. This is when you see images in your mind's eye (the 3rd eye). When you first begin, it may feel like just your imagination, but don't let that stop you from expressing it.

Clairaudience means clear hearing. We hear words, sounds or music in our mind's voice. It sometimes comes in a spontaneous thought that is not ours.

Clairsentience means clear feeling. We feel a person's or a spirit's emotions or physical pain. This may be expressed as "gut feeling" – or energy that makes the hair on the back of our neck stand up.

Claircognizance means clear knowing. This is when we have knowledge of people or events of which we would not normally have knowledge. For example, we know when someone is not telling the truth, or we know where the lost keys are.

Clairalience means clear smelling. We're able to smell odors that do not have a physical source.

Clairgustance means clear tasting – or the ability to taste something that isn't really there.

BUILDING A SPIRIT SYMBOL DICTIONARY

Mind, Body, Spirit – the names of our three bodies. Mind is consciousness. With our Physical Body we can touch and see and feel. The Spiritual body is our soul, a psychic being. It is our light, the body we've been discussing. Be aware and keep in mind that the Physical Body and Spirit Body cannot communicate directly. There is some sort of frequency or "veil" that does not permit them to communicate. So how do we get them to communicate? That's where the third body, which we call Consciousness, comes into play. It's our mental/emotional body.

All communications must go to and from the mental/emotional body. Since the spiritual body does not exist in this world it does not think like this world, so we have to find a way to communicate with it – and this is why we must create a "translation" book. I call it a Spirit Symbol Dictionary.

Because the spiritual body is not a "literal" being, it does not relate to calculations or formulas or directness. For this reason, when we want to communicate with the spiritual body, we must rely on feelings, images, and symbols. We build our bridge of communication via our mental/emotional body, and as with any other 'building project' this one requires time, labor, and consistency of effort.

STAY BALANCED

Finding balance within the self is key. I have seen many people start their spiritual path and not stay balanced –because they jump in so strong with the spiritual that they fail to take care of body or mind. They become overweight or "space headed." They burn out and end up so off-balance they cannot reach their true potential. Keep in mind that there is no finish line. Achieving balance is the goal, but there no reason to race ahead full steam. You're not competing with anyone.

WORKING WITH YOUR LIGHT

When you start "working with your light" you activate it. As you begin activating it you are actually saying you are willing to grow spiritually. All of us have the same amount of light, but some people dim their light. They may not be in touch with their spiritual side (soul) and do not care to "shine." That is a personal choice and chosen path. When we do choose to grow spiritually we are also choosing to connect with our soul. When we activate (or brighten) our light, that action/intention begins heightening our psychic ability.

BASIC PSYCHIC PROTECTION

You may ask why you need psychic protection. Is becoming a psychic dangerous? Well, there is a reason why psychics are labeled sensitive. I'm not a big fan of labels but the label "sensitive" does fit. Until you are strong in your abilities and become "aware," you will not need to create protection or practice protection. We psychics are rightfully labeled sensitive, because as we start reading, feeling, seeing, and working with energy we do become more sensitive to all forms of energy – and this includes negative and lower vibration energy. Emotions such as sadness, anxiety and depression –these are the low vibration energy and it can in the beginning make us feel a little moody or emotional. Let me add that this is just one example. So how can you protect yourself?

- **Know yourself - your emotions, your thoughts, your actions.** If you are feeling great and your mood swings suddenly, go within to see if the feeling is yours. If it's not yours, push it aside. You do this by imagining: *It is being whisked away by the wind.*
- **Shield yourself in a situation**. If you are in a large group or a situation that can be overwhelming, imagine being shielded: a white shield surrounds you, like the shell of an egg. It blocks out all negative and fear-based energy.

- **Psychic checks.** If you feel you have something negative attached to you, relax by taking a couple deep, slow breaths. Imagine scanning your body slowly with light, like a copier scan. Scan for dark spots. If there are dark spots, you have picked up negative energies. Do not panic. We psychics often pick up negative energies, but we use the light from the heart chakra – and make that light bigger and brighter and hot like a fire. That light burns off the dark spots and renews the light in our heart chakras. I recommend the practice of renewing the heart chakra's light each day. It feels good – and gets us really in touch with our light.

- **Feed your light.** Every morning, as I wake up, I lie in bed and tune into my light and imagine connecting with it. I close my eyes and take slow deep breaths. With every intake of breath I imagine pulling light (vital essence) from Mother Nature and from everywhere around me, and feeding it into my light, which is held in my heart chakra. As I do this I see my light getting bigger, brighter and lighter until it fills the room. Once my light is "full" and awake, I bring it back into my body and into my heart chakra. This helps me connect with Source, so I've protected myself and now feel charged for the day.

THE DIVINE TRINITY OF ENERGY:

Father/ Source

Let's switch gears now and talk about God/Source. God is the Source – the Source of all energy. I was raised Roman Catholic and we were taught the doctrine of the Trinity – that God has three parts: Father, Son, and Holy Spirit. When I attended Delphi University's Spiritual/Metaphysical School, I found that they used a similar analogy. They taught the Trinity of Energy. Source is the "Father" of all energy – the energy from which all things derive. Everything is energy, so everything is made of Source.

The Son: Substance / Divine Masculine

The second part of the trinity is the "Son" – also known as the Divine Masculine. Everything that is matter is the "Son" energy (the Divine Masculine). It is the earth, sun, trees, plants, woman, man, etc. It is energy, but condensed energy. Matter, on the other hand, is just matter, and has no life.

Holy Spirit / Divine Feminine / Life Force

This portion of the trinity is "spirit energy" (also called the Divine Feminine). She breathes life into everything, and is also known as vital essence or Prana). This spirit energy is the 'aliveness' that animates and flows through the trees, flowers, rivers, air, animals and you and me, etc. It is the life force that revitalizes everything. It connects us with everything on this planet and beyond. It is part of the Oneness. Call it Holy Spirit/ Spirit/Prana/Vital Essence. It is the fluid life force or cosmic energy that flows through everything and connects all. Spirit is all around us and in us. She is the Prana, the vital essence that makes everything alive.

The Divine Trinity / Unity

This is the unity, because it is the same flowing energy. This is how we can get information from all things.

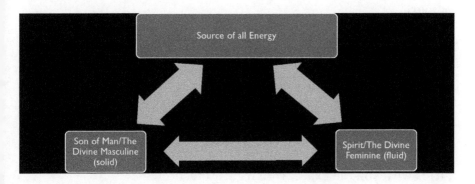

PSYCHIC BREATH

There is a way to learn and start to feel the connection with Spirit. It is called the Psychic Breath. Here is what you would imagine it would look like, and instructions on how to do the Psychic Breath.

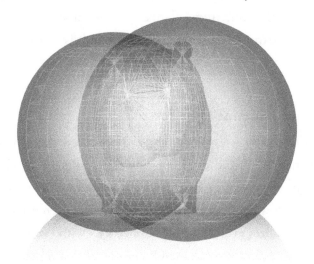

Imagine taking the Prana into your feet. Now allow it to flow into the body, up, up, up into the body slowly (count of four). Once it reaches your heart chakra, hold your breath (two seconds). That is where your light is held (spirit/soul). Allow the Prana to feed your light/spirit. Second by second the Prana makes your light grow bigger and brighter than your body. After the two seconds, slowly release the breath and allow the prana to continue to flow upward into your head and out your crown (count of four).

Continue this at least two more times.

Do this at least three times a day until you feel the connection. By 'feel' I mean you will actually feel sensation in your body, usually within 2-3 weeks (give or take). Then you can start doing it less or more, depending on how you choose. I do this before every reading and throughout the day. When you practice Psychic Breath day after day you grow and grow. Here's what you can expect with regular practice:

1. Prana practice feeds your vital essence and gives you energy.

2. It connects you with Spirit.

3. By pulling Prana through your feet, you are pulling it from Mother Nature so it helps to ground you.

4. It travels up your spine and opens and balances all the chakras.

5. It feeds your light.

6. It connects your light with Spirit.

7. As it travels through the crown chakra it travels up to God – and connects you to Source.

8. You become the channel to higher Wisdom.

9. You are protected because you are pulling in the White Light of Spirit.

PSYCHIC ENERGY BALL

Now that you are connected to Spirit, you can practice controlling energy. Here is a fun exercise that many psychics start with. You create a psychic energy ball with your hands. Begin by sitting comfortably, relaxed. After doing your usual Psychic Breath practice, go back to regular breathing and slightly rub your hands together for a couple seconds. Then place them apart about three inches. Your hands have to be in front of you, touching only the air. Look at your hands and imagine your light from your heart chakra lighting up and flowing down your shoulders and arms into your hands.

See the light create a ball of energy between your hands. You should feel a slight pull and push from the middle, like magnets in reverse. This is your energy – and the more you hold it the stronger it will feel. Play with it. Stretch it and pull it. Imagine it getting bigger. The more you practice the stronger you get at mastering control of psychic energy. Congratulations!

UNDERSTANDING YOUR INTUITION

It's very important that you understand your intuition. Remember that there is no wrong way – except holding back and not trying. So open up your mind and let it flow. You can't buy a book that will tell you what your intuition is telling you. Each of us is unique, so each one of us must go within to understand. We must ask for guidance about what things mean.

How can you understand what you are feeling? The answer is, 'Know thyself!" If you feel something but are unsure about it, take a few deep breaths and speak to self. "What does this mean to me?" Then stay real still, and you will likely get the answer. I tell my students to become again the 4-year-old and go within – and keep on asking questions until you do understand. Understanding gut feelings and emotions is of utmost importance. You must learn to trust your gut and your emotions. If physical sensitivity, pain, or illness appears suddenly and often – and also disappears often, rest assured that this is a symptom of Clairsentience. You are picking up other people's pain and sickness. Your task/aim is to understand your body and its warnings, so go within and ask, "Is this my pain?"

If you get the feeling it isn't, then you can keep asking. "Whose energy is it? Why am I feeling it? What do I need to know?" And etc.

A lot of people don't trust themselves when they are first developing because it is difficult to distinguish the difference between Spirit and imagination. At first they feel similar. The more you practice and work with them, the more obvious the difference becomes. How do I understand what I am seeing? Symbols, shapes, or math equations? The same advice applies. Go within and ask, "What does this mean?" And you will get guidance.

INTUITIVE COLORS

Let's talk about intuitive colors. John Russell said, *"Color is energy made visible."* Intuitive colors are different from Chakra and Aura colors, Intuitive colors are personal colors that mean something to you. You may have heard descriptions like, "I am so angry I am seeing red." Or, "He is green with envy." There are books and websites on intuitive colors, but no book or website can tell you how your intuition should be. For example, what red means to you may mean something different to me. Why? You might like red, but I personally don't care for it. If I see someone and the color red flashes in my mind's eye, that might not be a good thing. This could be the opposite for you, it could be your favorite color and red flashes in your mind's eye, then it would be good for you.

The following quote about light and color says it well. *"The source of all color is light. Without light, there is no color. Light is the messenger and color is the message. Leonardo da Vinci observed that color does not exist without light, and was criticized by his peers for such radical thoughts. Robert Boyle, a seventeenth-century English physicist, concluded that colors are diversified light. Isaac Newton demystified the relationship between color and light by passing sunlight through a triangular glass prism and he saw that the rays of white light were bent or refracted, spreading out like a fan. He called the resulting range of colors a spectrum: red, orange, yellow, green, blue, indigo, and violet."* (McCartney, 2005)

And below I've listed examples of intuitive colors – positive and negative – from a website: http://www.empower-yourself-with-color-psychology.com/

Red: Positive keywords include: action, energy and speed, attention-getting, assertive and confident, energizing, stimulating, exciting, powerful, passionate, stimulating and driven, courageous and strong, spontaneous and determined.

Negative keywords include: aggressive and domineering, over-bearing, tiring, angry and quick-tempered, ruthless, fearful and intolerant, rebellious and obstinate, resentful, violent and brutal.

Orange: Positive keywords include: sociable, optimistic, enthusiastic, cheerful, self-confident, independent, flamboyant, extroverted and uninhibited, adventurous, the risk-taker, creative flair, warm-hearted, agreeable and informal.

Negative keywords include: superficial and insincere, dependent, over-bearing, self-indulgent, the exhibitionist, pessimistic, inexpensive, unsociable, and overly proud.

Yellow: Positive keywords include: optimism, cheerfulness, enthusiasm, fun, good-humored, confidence, originality, creativity, challenging, academic and analytical, wisdom and logic.

Negative keywords include: being critical and judgmental, being overly analytical, being impatient and impulsive, being egotistical, pessimistic, an inferiority complex, spiteful, cowardly, deceitful, non-emotional and lacking compassion.

Green: Positive keywords include: growth and vitality, renewal and restoration, self-reliance, reliability and dependability, being tactful, emotionally balanced and calm, nature lover and family oriented, practical and down to earth, sympathetic, compassionate and nurturing, generous, kind and loyal with a high moral sense, adaptable, encourages 'social joining' of clubs and other groups, a need to belong.

Negative keywords include: being possessive and materialistic, indifferent and over-cautious, envious, selfish, greedy and miserly, devious with money, inconsiderate, inexperienced, a hypochondriac and a do-gooder.

Blue: Positive keywords include: loyalty, trust and integrity, tactful, reliability and responsibility, conservatism and perseverance, caring and concern, idealistic and orderly, authority, devotion and contemplation, peaceful and calm.

Negative keywords include: being rigid, deceitful and spiteful, depressed and sad, too passive, self-righteous, superstitious and emotionally unstable, too conservative and old-fashioned, predictable and weak, unforgiving, aloof and frigid. It can also indicate manipulation, unfaithfulness and being untrustworthy.

Purple: Positive keywords include: unusual and individual, creative and inventive, psychic and intuitive, humanitarian, selfless and unlimited, mystery, fantasy and the future.

Negative keywords include: immature, practical, cynical and aloof, pompous and arrogant, fraudulent and corrupt, delusions of grandeur, and social climber.

[A personal comment on the above. In my opinion, if you add white to any color it raises the vibration of the color. Blue, for example. Light blue becomes peaceful and calm, which translates to tranquility. Purple transmutes to violet and becomes spiritual, intuitive.]

Pink: Unconditional love. Inhaling pink or white and exhaling green will keep your energy at its highest level and soothe the soul. The pink in the air is vital essence (Prana/Spirit) in the air. You can heal yourself through meditation and creative visualization.

Hot Pink/Fuchsia A new relationship. That lusty butterfly can't wait to see your love.

CHAPTER 8

EMPOWERING THE EMPATH WITHIN

IF BY NOW YOU'VE IDENTIFIED yourself as an Empath or know someone who is an Empath, or if you're not quite ready to admit you are or can be an Empath, keep reading. It's time to go a little deeper. I've shared with you my struggles as I grew up – the agony of trying to understand my abilities, and how I came to understand that burdens usually turn out to be blessings. I know now that I needed those struggles. They forced me to understand my desire for knowledge and my empathic abilities.

The lessons and struggles also made me appreciate and connect with people on a deeper level. Connecting with another on an emotional level creates one of the strongest of bonds, so I now do this many times throughout the day and give much gratitude for it. Another incredible thing about being an Empath is that when we "master" our abilities and find peace within self, we can project emotions. This may sound a little radical – but remember that at the stage of mastery you are at the Divine phase of being an Empath. At that stage you radiate divine love. Imagine stepping into a room full of tension or anger and being able to project peace and harmony. You feel the tension in the room dissipate. What a blessing to be able to create love and harmony. First though, you must attain that mastery phase. In this chapter I go deeper into the three phases of becoming an Empath. You can continue to grow into your next phase, and as your skills widen you will then find yourself fluctuating in and out of the three phases.

PHASE ONE – THE UNSKILLED EMPATH

Perhaps you have wondered if you are an Empath. Or maybe you feel what an Empath feels but don't know why (as I did, in the beginning). Maybe you've never even heard the term 'Empath' yet when in the company of another you pick up on that individual's emotions. If you're still wondering, consider the following questions.

Do others see you as moody or a loner—due to the downtime you need?

Do you feel the emotions of others and take them on as your own?

Do you pick up 'sympathy pains' – the physical symptoms of others, especially those you're closest to?

Do you suffer digestive disorders and lower back pain?

Do your relationships often move too fast and/or become intense very quickly?

An Empath is a human being who feels the feelings and emotions of other human beings. But it's not quite that simple. An Empath also *absorbs* the other's emotions. Imagine going through life like that! It wouldn't be so bad if it were just one other person, or one person once in a while, or even one at a time. It takes a toll on your emotions and on your body. This is why many Empaths seclude themselves. They have to, in order to "recharge." Common physical symptoms for those with Empathic powers include stomach problems, back pain, chronic fatigue syndrome, fibromyalgia, and arthritis.

Most people don't realize the difference between experiencing empathy and being an Empath, so let me explain. While every human has at least the potential ability to feel some empathy for others, in our entire population only an estimated 2% are Empaths, or healers.

If someone tells of experiencing something extremely difficult or sad – you will perhaps feel sad for that person. We call that 'empathy.' But an Empath may wake up in the morning feeling wonderful and decide to stop for a cup of coffee and someone in the coffee shop is extremely depressed. Though the Empath does not even encounter the person, simply walking into the building has the Empath feeling and absorbing the depressed individual's emotions – so immediately this inexperienced Empath is depressed. The difficulty here is that the depression can last for weeks, because the immature Empath is unaware of his or her powers and therefore doesn't even know why depression has settled in.

The Empath has an intuitive ability, and the ability can be trained and developed. This individual can live a life that is not a rollercoaster of emotions, but first there must be recognition of the gift. Yes, the power must be recognized. When fully developed, the empathic power is the ability to heal.

If you are an Empath there are many traits of it you need to understand, and in this modern world you simply can go to the Internet and find multiple websites for researching the subject.

I remember well that feeling of being alone and being different. I was labeled so many things I started to believe there was something wrong with me. But there wasn't anything wrong. There was something right! I had this gift. I was an Empath.

If by now you have identified yourself as an Empath you probably are feeling what I call the "burden" or "curse" of this ability to pick up on other people's feelings. It is the first of three phases. I call the first the **Unskilled Empath.** You recognize that you are an Empath, and you relate to some or most of the traits. Life at this point is difficult and may even seem a burden. It's a struggle to get through everyday life – but it's also time to start researching how to create shielding to protect your self. To recharge, you have to go into seclusion.

Second phase is the **Empowered Empath**. Now you've begun to accept your gift, even appreciate it. You don't blame the world or anyone else for the energy that is coming through. You are becoming more open and compassionate with your feelings because it doesn't hurt so much. You are feeling empowered, in control, no longer afraid of your abilities. You are allowing it to flow more freely. However, there are days that it can still be a little overwhelming, but not nearly as much and you have learned to release it much faster. You still feel the need to shield yourself and guard. The fun part of this phase is discovering your abilities and the "type of empath" – and what you can really do.

If you have now realized that you relate to most of the traits of an Empath, you may find the realization a burden. And you blame the world. Your ability seems a curse and makes just getting through the day a struggle. You find yourself needing to seclude yourself to recharge. You blame others for negative feelings you experience, or unknowingly hold emotions of others in your energy field – which makes you want to shut yourself down.

You are exhausted and almost ready to give up, though in actuality this is the time to learn how to create shielding to protect the self. I understand – because I've been there. Up to this point in your life you have been experiencing something you just don't quite understand. You can't see it. And it doesn't align with the understanding of those around you, so you feel as though you are a victim of your psychic ability. And the people you care about feel sorrowful for you – but they have underestimated you! Time has come to take charge of your ability and discover how wonderful it can be. Time has come for you to *discover your power* and take charge of your life.

First off, you must redefine who you are. Do you really know who you are? Or are you losing yourself in everyone else's emotions? Ask yourself, "How smart am I?" We're not talking book smart here. Society may judge you that way, but I'm here to remind you that you are not the "average norm." I'm here to tell you that you are something more: you are a "sensitive." By the time you finish reading this chapter you will understand what I mean, but I can tell you right now that what you are is incredible.

Society will tell you how beautiful you are, how nice you are and what you are good or bad at. But be careful. Do not let anyone dictate to you who you are. Chances are, you don't know the real you! Teachers and bosses and parents will tell you who you are, and hopefully those judgments are paired with love, but even so, what these folks have said has not served "the authentic you." But now, time has come – the time for shifting your perception and discovering your true self.

Nikola Tesla was an inventor and physicist, and a genius when it came to work with electrical power. Energy and frequency were things he knew well. Tesla saw everything as energy and frequency. He said that when we look around the room everything we see is matter – but matter is only 2% of the energy around us. The other 98% may be invisible to the eye, but *it is* energy. That 98% has vibration (frequency), which means it carries "information." I get his work, though I don't understand half the information intellectually. I do though understand that everything is energy, 2% visible, 98% not.

Your whole life you've been told that you're too sensitive. Or too intense, too emotional. And now here I am to tell you that for your whole life you've been handed a misperception. As a 'sensitive' you've been picking up on the 98% of the energy that most people cannot pick up on. For example…ever walked into a room and found the odor extremely potent? And the longer people remain there, the less they smell it? That's called *sensory adaption.*

Sensory adaption allows people to adapt to their environment, while balancing the need to receive new sensory input. The odor being transmitted is energy, but with most people the longer they're subjected to the odor, the more their ability to 'smell' is dulled or numbed. Most people are not sensitive enough to feel the energy, but as a 'sensitive' you are able to smell it. This is a normal thing with you – too sensitive, while others are dull to the phenomena. This is an example of what I'm talking about when I speak of shifting your perspective about yourself.

Let's talk more about energy, or to be exact, spiritual energy. I define spiritual energy as the energy that binds the soul (spirit) to our body. It is our breath of life, our *chi*, our prana. We receive and transmit this spiritual energy through our chakras and our meridians. Our spiritual energy surrounds us. It is commonly known as our aura, but I want you to understand that it is so much more.

As an Empath, you need to understand how to store, preserve and transmit spiritual energy. This point is key to mastering your abilities. Humans are energy transformers who transmit an energy field, an individual unit of power. The better we transmit this energy or allow it to flow through us, the more refined our experience of life and the higher our awareness. Psychics refer to it as raising our vibration. The higher our vibration, the more alive, contented and effective we become. The Universe is a web of energy conveying life force.

All entities (humans, animals, plants, spirits, etc.) within this network receive and transmit energy through radiation. We receive and transmit spiritual, psychic, and physical energy in direct relation to our developing intellectual and spiritual capabilities. As we learn to *attune our selves* to the universal energy frequency, we experience spiritual and psychic entrainment.

The more you study and do your spiritual practice, the more your vibration will increase to receive spiritual energy. And the more psychic practice work you do, the more your vibration will increase to receive psychic energy and so on.

One of the foundations of most education is 'perennialism,' a philosophy used in our educational system. Perennialists are philosophers, educators, scientists, etc. Aristotle, Socrates and Plato were perennialists.

They believed students should study the great works of old to learn "the perennial wisdom" – in other words, the wisdom of the ages, those timeless wisdoms that were as true thousands of years ago as they are now and shall be in future. These truths have withstood the test of time. All students should study them to gain understanding of the philosophical concepts that underlie human knowledge.

Perennialists believe that God (Higher Power/Source) and education go together, hand in hand, and that education is the foundational preparation with which a person gleans the truth from life experience. Perennialists believe that a relationship to a spiritual being (God/Source) is necessary for understanding the cosmos or universe. Perennialism includes the philosophies of idealism, realism, and neo-theism – and holds to the belief that environment plays a big role in teaching an individual.

You may wonder why I elaborate on Perennialism. I find it to be an effective way of speaking about energy – or more precisely, how we can understand and preserve energy. We use energy in different forms, including electricity, magnetism, microwaves and electromagnetic waves. Seers within the Perennial tradition preserve and use spiritual energy. This subtle form of energy operates according to specific principles, so it is essential that we learn these principles – so we can practice them. For Empaths, this knowledge is of extra importance. Just as electricity can potentially be deadly if handled by a person ignorant of its power, so spiritual energy can also be misused and cause harm.

How many times have you felt an overabundance of depression, anxiety and sadness – then realized it was not yours? Like all other emotions these too are energy, but energy at a low vibration – so do keep in mind that *the Perennial tradition focuses on elevating energy*. Spiritual energy can be directed by concentrated focus, such as prayer and spiritual healing. Perennialist meditation focuses and transmits spiritual energy – directing it to a specific destination for a specific purpose.

Since external and internal energy focal points affect our bodies, minds, and our states of consciousness, we must carefully select the inputs we allow into our experience. Keep in mind that chakra balancing, exercise, play, and meditation are key factors to a healthy life. Here's a list of some other things that affect us:

- **Thoughts** - What we think creates, thus positive thoughts are very important.

- **Feelings** - Allow your self to feel deeply without guilt or self-judgment, and then consciously release these feelings.

- **Images** - What you see in negative images in magazines and film can be embedded in the subconscious, thus the need for a neutralizing perspective.

- **Sounds** - What we listen to, such as music. Are you listening to the uplifting and positive?

- **Written material** - What we read affects our view on life – either corrupts or enhances.

- **People** – Those we choose to permit into our surroundings can definitely change our perception.

- **Activities** - Exercise and stimulation for the body, and creative hobbies – all extremely important.

- **Food and Liquids** - We sometimes engage the habit of emotional eating. Alcohol, meats, gluten, GMO and processed foods are extremely toxic for the emotional state of an Empath. Because we are energy sensitive, we must give attention to making adjustments in our habits. The items listed affect our state of being more than you can imagine. My suggestion is that you go without one of these items for two weeks and monitor how you feel. You will likely be shocked.

Every time we interact with another person, we exchange energy. Extensive interaction with individuals carrying negative energy may leave us with a build-up of harmful energy. *We must recognize negative energy and cleanse it from our field.* In this way we prevent physical, emotional, mental, and spiritual problems. Fortunately, the opposite is equally true. Spending time with positively charged persons helps us build and maintain our positive energy.

The way we view our self plays a major role. Do understand that it is possible for students of the Perennialist wisdoms (which we spoke of above) to overcome all aspects of the "debilitating self." In other words – it is possible to get rid of our sense of *self-importance*. We all need *frequent emphasis* on understanding self, so we must frequently take inventory of our psychic and spiritual energies. The goal is to avoid the patterns those self-important energies make in us as they give away energy without regard. Your goal becomes to learn to store your energy, so it can transform your self.

One of our greatest enemies is the sense of self-importance. We allow ourselves to be weakened by feeling offended by the deeds and misdeeds of other people. We have been taught that self-importance requires us to spend most of our lives being accepted or offended by someone. This relates back to what I was talking about earlier: allowing others to tell us who we are. It's way past time to change this harmful habit. Our goal must be to store energy, no longer permit any person or thing to take it from us. You will find some individuals attacking you and directing negative energy toward you. They may want to start a verbal fight, or yell at you or offend you. If you counterattack, all you accomplish is using your body's energy against the other. By engaging the attack, you waste your energy in a force-against-force battle.

Instead, try the alternative. As the attacker pushes against you, step to the side and let the other's negative momentum throw him or her off-balance. In this way the other person uses up energy while you use very little. What you've done is allow that person to play the fool. Perennialists called this scenario, "Spiritual Judo." As I was teaching this in a class a student asked, "Why would you leave your foot out?" The answer is simple. Because I am not a doormat. We can be kind and spiritual, but this does not mean we should be walked over or pushed around. A very old saying puts it this way: "Give them enough rope and they will hang themselves."

I want to recommend an exercise that will help you understand yourself and other people. It's an excellent way of releasing emotional attachments to your old belief systems about your self. Remember that everyone is a mirror, or reflection. Think of the three people you are closest to. Write their names on a piece of paper. In a column, list ten qualities you love about them and then circle the top three qualities – the ones you love best. Then on a separate piece of paper name three people who really bother you – and be honest. Again, in a column, list ten qualities you don't like about these people. Then circle the three qualities you most dislike.

In both exercises you can count the three traits you selected as *your qualities*. This exercise is called a "mirror" because it permits you to see your reflection. Though you may not have said it precisely, you will understand what you're getting at, and the more you do the exercise the more you will understand others and yourself. It will eventually help you see and change your perspective on why someone makes you feel a certain way. No one "makes" you feel a certain way. You feel a certain way because you recognize qualities in others that are particular to you. I am here to stress the value of paying close attention to how interactions with others make you feel. This is a prime means toward understanding your own individual self.

Now let's talk about energy. What is energy? Energy is movement, vibration, frequency. Energy is sound, light, color, emotions, feelings. Energy is life – and therefore energy is Spirit. We are energy and everything is made up of energy. Every sound has a different frequency or tone. Every frequency resonates with a vibration. Every color and emotion has a vibration – the higher the frequency, the shorter the wavelength.

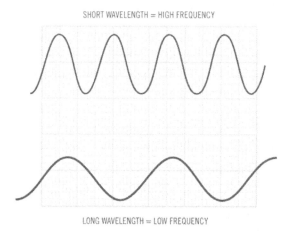

The color violet is high frequency. Laughter and soft music are high frequencies. The lower frequencies have the longer wavelength. The color red is low frequency. Sadness, yelling and fighting are low frequencies.

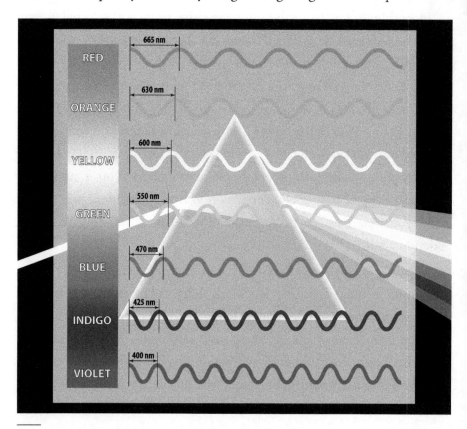

Let's talk more specifically about feelings and emotions. Is there a difference? Absolutely. And if you look up those words, in most modern dictionaries they seem to be synonyms. But there is a difference – though to put that difference in words is difficult. A feeling is a mental energy affecting your thoughts. An emotion is more physical and affects your entire body. For example, someone says something and it makes you angry. You know anger is an emotion because you feel it with every fiber of your being. It makes you want to lash back and say something hurtful. Or you may want to scream or cry. The energy of the emotion affects the entire body.

One way to handle a powerful negative energy is to channel that energy in a positive way. Decide to clean your house with that energy. Have you ever cleaned your house when you are angry? I strongly recommend it – for it is a positive way of releasing negative energy. The energy behind the emotion (anger, in this case) dissipates because you have unleashed your wrath on your house in a positive way. Now that you have calmed down, you can discuss the situation with the person that upset you rationally. That emotion has now become a feeling. The energy behind it has been released and is now more of a mental problem. Remember that emotions are feelings with energy behind them.

Even the human body has a frequency. A healthy human frequency lies within the range of 62-72 Hz. When the human frequency drops to lower levels it enables the appearance of a variety of diseases. For example, at the level of 58 Hz, diseases like cold and flu are more likely to appear. On much lower levels (42 Hz) cancer may appear. Here are examples of human frequencies.

- Shame = 20
- Feeling guilty = 30
- Apathy = 50
- Grief = 75
- Fear = 100

- Desire = 125
- Anger = 150
- Vanity = 175
- Boldness = 200
- Neutrality = 250
- Readiness = 310
- Adoption = 350
- Mind = 400
- Love = 500
- Joy = 540
- Harmony = 600
- Enlightenment = 700+

When we change our perspective and grow, we allow ourselves to expand. This is what we call raising our vibration, but *limiting your perspective* will lower your vibration and slow your frequency. Other examples of how we lower our vibration include junk food, and processed foods, wanting more rather than being grateful for what we have, gossiping about others, living in the past, worrying about the future, alcohol and drugs, negative self-talk and not feeling 'good enough,' toxic products, toxic environment (think cosmetics, cleaners, pollution etc.), and prolonged exposure to electronics, cell phones, computers and TV, and also holding on to anger, guilt, or resentment. And we must also factor in stress and anxiety.

Conversely, some things raise our vibrations. These include meditation, creativity, eating raw/whole foods, focusing on gratitude, feeling unconditional love, being in nature, crystals, accepting what is, yoga/exercise, laughing, and musical activities.

More Vibration Facts:

- Negative thoughts lower your vibrational frequency by 12mhz.
- Positive thoughts raise your vibrational frequency by 10mhz.

- Prayer and meditation raise vibrational frequency by 15mhz.
- Processed/canned food - 0mhz
- Fresh produce - up to 15mhz
- Dry herbs - 12 to 22mhz
- Fresh herbs - 20-27mhz
- Essential oils - 52-320mhz

PHASE TWO: THE SKILLED EMPATH

In the second stage – you feel empowered. You have redefined yourself and are starting to accept the gift. You can recognize and feel the energy as it comes in and you don't blame anyone for what they are feeling. You are more open, showing compassion and love for everyone. You know you are in control, and you are no longer in fear of being an Empath. One of the nice things about this is that there are ten different types of empaths. As you release old beliefs and patterns of what you think of your self, you find there is no need to keep to your old boundaries.

Yes, you may at times still feel overwhelmed, but you are learning to deal with it more quickly. You know you cannot shield yourself from your empathic abilities. You may feel the emotions of others, but you have learned the skills to deal with it. You have stopped blaming others for their merges with you.

TEN TYPES OF EMPATHS:

1. **Claircognizant Empath** - This type of Empath is typically defined by the capacity to know something must be done, or whether something is true or deceptive, though there may not be any basis for it in reason or logic. Most often this type of Empath knows when someone is lying or hiding something, or when something is right or not. Some people believe Claircognizance is given to us

by spirit guides, angels, or through contact with one's own higher self. They believe this information is accessed through a person's Crown Chakra. Others assert that this information is taken from what is called the Akashic Records. Those who are Claircognizant tend to be people who are cognitive, cerebral and/or analytical by nature. They may engage automatic writing, intuitive painting, playing an instrument intuitively, and psychic readings.

2. **Emotionally Sensitive Empath** - Many Empaths tend to be emotionally sensitive and feel another individual's emotions both emotionally and physically before it is expressed. When dealing with energy healing, you will be dealing with the emotions of others, so you never want to take on their feelings. Therefore, state that intention! Visualize the color and pull out the energy of the emotion, not the feeling. This is a form of energy healing.

3. **Physically Sensitive Empath** - Many Empaths tend to be physically open to bodily pains and other people's sicknesses. This can be an especially useful ability in healing, and does frequently show itself in the Empath's body.

4. **Fauna Empath** - This type of Empath can feel, hear and communicate with animals, though differently than an animal communicator or a vegan would. Not all animal communicators are Fauna Empaths, but all Fauna Empaths are animal communicators. Not all vegans are Fauna Empaths, but all Fauna Empaths *should be* vegans. Working with animals enhances this empath's ability to grow. It's good to visualize colors, pictures, moods – and "pulling out" the low vibration energy that is not needed.

5. **Flora Empath** - This Empath connects with plants and receives signals that are mental and/or physical by connecting with the vibrations of plants – such as color and smell. They can raise the vibration of the room with the plants as they meditate and

communicate with them. Try making essential oil, tinctures, herbs, etc.

6. **Geomantic Empath** – A Geomantic Empath is a reader of the energy of Planet Earth. Many are able to predict and feel natural disasters before they happen. You may find yourself either uncomfortable or really happy in certain environments or situations – for no apparent reason. You may be drawn to sacred stones, groves, churches or other places of sacred power. You may also be sensitive to the history of a place and able to pick up on sadness, fear or joy that has occurred in certain locations. Choose natural materials, such as wood and linen for your clothing and furniture.

7. **Psychometric Empath** - This Empath has the ability to receive information, impressions and energy from physical items like clothes, photographs, jewelry etc. Follow these simple steps: 1. Ask someone to bring you a few small objects with which you can practice. 2. It's good in the beginning if the objects are small enough to fit in your hands. Jewelry and keys are great, as metal holds energy well. A piece of jewelry that has been worn a lot (such as a wedding ring) will have more energy than something that is rarely used. 3. Sit comfortably and take a few deep breaths. Rub your hands together a few times to get the energy moving. You may feel a tingling sensation in your hands. 4. Take the object in your hands and close your eyes. Continue to relax and take note of how your body feels. Do you feel, see or hear anything? If not, it's okay, there's no right or wrong. If you feel stuck, try asking yourself some questions: Does this object belong to a man or a woman? Is the owner of this object happy or sad? Does this person have any children? What kind of work does this person do? 5. Write down everything you see, hear and feel, even if it seems silly. Don't filter anything. The point of this exercise is to get you used to receiving energetic impressions. If you are working with

a partner, share your impressions. 6. When you are done, ask the person who gave you the object to give you feedback. You want to know if they can validate the things you felt, saw, or heard.

8. **Precognitive Empath** - This kind of Empath can feel the occurrence of a situation or an event before it happens. You experience precognitive dreams. If you feel anxious, or experience visions prior to a major event taking place, or seem to know when a pet, a friend or a loved one is in trouble – you may be tapping into your "precog" abilities. You may have a sense of déjà vu. You have exceptionally fine-tuned perceptions of energy, or vibrations. You can pick up on the energy in a room or building where a major event took place.

9. **Telepathic Empath** - This Empath can read a person's unexpressed thoughts. Ask a friend or relative who is not a skeptic to help you by focusing on a picture or object. Then try to focus on their thoughts and pick up whatever is being seen. It's best if whatever is being looked at is able to evoke a powerful emotion, whether strong admiration, excitement, anger or other strong feeling. This creates stronger waves of energy, so you'll be able to pick up on it easier. Relax your mind and try not to think too hard about picking up on what the other person is thinking or feeling. Concentration is actually counterproductive, since your mind must be open to receive whatever signals are being emitted.

10. **Medium Empath** - This Empath can see, hear, and feel spirits – typically from dead individuals.

PHASE THREE: THE ENLIGHTENED EMPATH

This Empath has mastered the gift of radiating divine love. By merging conscious effort with love this one has the ability to easily heal others – because this Empath is no longer contaminated by the fears and negativity of others and can therefore transform and transmute fear – simply by being present. The personal life of this Empath is dedicated only to what the Divine asks of him or her.

CHAPTER 9

CONCLUSION - AWAKENING ENERGY AND DAILY ROUTINE

THE AWAKENING

Recently there is a process occurring that many people are hearing about. The Awakening or Spiritual Awakening, which means that one's soul is waking up and no longer wants to live in the darkness of lower vibrations such as judgment, hate, avarice and self-aggrandizement. The soul no longer wants to live in an egoic system built on the philosophy, "What's in it for me?" or "What will society think of me?"

This "awakening" is a call to a higher purpose. It's true, yes, that we are all individuals and have different paths in life. I want to stress here the fact that there are very few blanket statements I dare to make, but this that I make now is one. We all have the same higher purpose, though not the same path. There's a difference. Our higher purpose is to connect into the Oneness. How do we do this? The answer is clear: through love. In all the ancient Wisdom Traditions we are told to love each other, help each other and be in service to help connect through love. How each of us finds that connection is (of course) individualized – and is our life's path.

TRIGGERS

You may remember from earlier pages that my back issues triggered my awakening. Looking back, I can see that it was as if my soul was screaming for my attention. That is, of course, not how everyone experiences a call to attention. It does not have to be so extreme. It may be spontaneous, or may be triggered by something like a paranormal experience (near death, UFO, ghost), or by a   major life event such as a death in the family or divorce or loss of job. At this moment many people are experiencing this "call to attention."

And then there are others who search for the truth or may be led to it by a specific event, a video, book or movie. Lastly, there are those who were born awakened.

The awakening process serves many purposes. I list here the ones most common. To discover purpose or life calling; to learn to fully love self and others; to connect with the spiritual self (the light); to raise consciousness and thereby raise the consciousness of the planet; to explore, expand and discover higher levels of the inner self; to discover the psychic/spiritual abilities in order to help self and others; to connect with Source and other living things on this planet and beyond; to fully experience life; to forgive self and develop a deeper level of sensitivity (empathy, compassion, pure heart). All of these and more are effects of Awakening.

Many people are now awakening and becoming aware of their spiritual path. They are coming to understand that their psychic being and psychic abilities are becoming aligned – and that this alignment leads to wholeness. If you are experiencing any of the following symptoms without cause – do not be alarmed. Do be aware that you are going through the awakening process.

SYMPTOMS OF A SPIRITUAL AWAKENING

Physical Symptoms

1. Tingling hands or feet.
2. Heart palpitations/racing heart.
3. Tingling in the third eye area (between the eyes).
4. Warm palms or feet.
5. Headaches, backaches, general aches and pains not caused by illness.
6. Changes in weight and eating habits.
7. Food intolerance and allergies that were not previously a problem.
8. Skin eruptions, rashes, itchy skin and tingling in the body.
9. Pain, numbness and feelings of vibration and electricity going through the body.
10. Dizzy spells and a feeling of lightness.
11. Feeling more tired and needing to rest a lot more than normal.
12. Memory loss and forgetfulness.
13. Changes in energy levels.
14. A feeling of waves of energy going through the body.
15. A feeling of brain fog.
16. Feelings of pressure inside the head, as though it might explode.
17. Night sweats.
18. Enhancement of physical senses, such as smell, sight and hearing.
19. Looking younger.
20. Hair and nails growing at a faster rate.
21. Changes in sleep patterns – restless sleep and/or waking up two or three times during the night.
22. Changes in bowel movements, perhaps bouts of diarrhea.
23. Sinus and ear trouble.

Emotional Symptoms

1. Sudden waves of emotions.
2. Sudden feelings of sadness then happiness, depression or elation.
3. A feeling of being on an emotional roller coaster ride.
4. Intense mood swings.
5. Suppressed and forgotten memories and old stuff resurfacing and causing waves of sad or happy emotions.
6. Emotional confusion.
7. Feelings of great joy and bliss.
8. Crying outbursts with no reason.
9. Wanting to withdraw from family and friends.
10. Feelings of loneliness, disconnection and being different from others.
11. Loss of motivation; feeling like not doing anything or that there's no point in doing anything.
12. Feeling irritable, angry and impatient.
13. Feeling as if your life is out of control and a mess.

Mental Symptoms

1. A sense of losing the mind.
2. A sense of going insane and losing control.
3. Feelings of fear.
4. Hearing voices that don't feel as if they're coming from within you.
5. Feeling at times like you are going crazy.

Spiritual/Psychic Symptoms

1. Dreams that are more vivid and intense. Spiritual dreams; dreams of angels, guides or deceased loved ones.

2. Sudden ability to hear and communicate with guides, angels or deceased loved ones.

3. Empathetic feelings and sensitivity toward the feelings of other people.

4. Questioning life and why you are here; intense feeling and the urge to find your life purpose.

5. A sudden feeling that you are different from friends and family.

6. The realization of what your life purpose is and how to fulfill it.

7. Synchronicity, and coincidences often occurring around you.

8. A feeling of being a different person to what you previously were – before awakening.

9. Paranormal activity; sensing of presences; seeing guides, angels, deceased loved ones and other spirit beings/spirit lights; a higher awareness of the spiritual world.

10. Feeling closer to animals and nature – and at one with everything.

11. Experiencing an intense urge to find your soul mate/twin flame.

12. Experiencing conscious and spontaneous out-of-body experiences (OBEs).

13. Experiencing a higher awareness or knowing when you perceive things.

14. Leaving behind friends you've outgrown and making new ones who feel the way you do now.

15. Seeing colors in your mind's eye and peripheral vision.

16. Becoming suddenly interested in healing, crystals, tarot cards and other divination aids and spiritual topics.

17. Starting to take better care of your body, and eating healthier and exercising more.

18. Becoming aware of psychic gifts, healing abilities and other gifts you previously were unaware of though you now find that you want to use them.

19. Experiencing a strong urge to spread awareness and share personal experiences with others – and to speak your truth.

20. Perhaps experiencing the blue pearl – a tiny blue dot seen in the mind's eye or peripheral vision or directly in front of you.

21. Finding that teachers or other people who can advise and help you with your spiritual journal suddenly turn up.

22. Experiencing an intense urge to discover spiritual truths because you yearn for meaning and purpose.

23. Wanting to break old habits and routines so you can engage more fulfilling things.

Whether you're going through the awakening process or want to enhance your psychic abilities, it is important to know one thing. LET GO! It is crucial that you relax, and let go of every expectation. You *are* energy, so you don't have to try to let it flow. Simply let it flow. It happens naturally.

Remember that your soul – your psychic being and your light – is an individualized expression of Source. Allow yourself to feel the flow of energy that is Spirit, the vital essence – the thing that animates all life. That flowing energy connects us all, and flows naturally – so you need to do nothing except be present and let it carry you.

If you honor the light within and honor the light in everything, you soon recognize that we are all the same. Love flows alongside the information.

I must stress the importance of creating a daily routine: your spiritual practice. In case it may help you, I provide here an example of my morning routine.

1. In the morning I wake up and connect with my light. Before even getting out of bed, I lie still and relax. Slowing my breath, I close my eyes and imagine my light. It is located within my heart chakra. I visualize it. With every breath, I breathe in light. I visualize my light getting bigger, brighter and warmer – until it fills the room. When the room is filled with light I bring the light back into my heart chakra and I'm ready to start the day.

Why is connecting with your light important? Because it clears all negativity and starts the day fresh. It will help you feel your power and your God-self, and connect you with Spirit. It also protects you with the white light of the Divine.

Here are a few other recommendations:

1. **Practice psychic breathing** at least three times a day.
2. **Control the energy** around you (psychic ball exercise).
3. **Practice Mindfulness** throughout the day.
4. **Exercise**. Yoga and Tai Chi are wonderful ways to enhance the energy flow.
5. **Do Visualization Exercises**. It is important to exercise your third eye. There is no specific way of doing this – it's your choice. And you can make it as complicated or as easy as you like. I visualize the energy and colors going through the third eye and practice visualizing energy around plants and people. I also like to visualize "cleaning" my pineal gland. Find a picture of the pineal gland and then imagine white energy clearing out all the hard calcification that builds up. The pineal gland is the connection to Source and your third eye, so clearing it is important.

6. **Meditate** – meditation is essential. Here are a couple of meditation ideas...

   a. Create a meditation.

   b. Clear the chakras - take one chakra at a time and work with it, make sure the energy is flowing properly and the color is perfect, then move to the next.

   c. Contemplation. Find a saying you like and sit with it, then go into meditation with the thought or saying and see what you get while in meditation.

   d. Present moment. Sit quietly in meditation. Focus on a particular part of your body and feel it. What does it tell you? When it is done, move on to the next part of your body. Continue this process until you have completed your entire body.

   e. Zen meditation – breath only. Clear your mind and just focus on your breath the entire time.

   f. Mantra/Affirmation - repeat a mantra or affirmation over and over during a meditation.

   g. White light surrounds you from above like an egg. Let the light heal and replenish you.

   h. Sound meditation. You can purchase music or go to a group sound-healing to experience many 'sound' healings.

   i. Guided meditation. There are many available CDs and videos geared toward taking you on a meditation journey.

   j. A bath – one of the most calming ways to meditate. Just relax and soak in the tub and be in the present moment.

2. **Get plenty of sleep.**

3. **De-stress.**

4. **Seek mental stimulation.**

5. **Get some sunlight.**

6. Eat a healthy diet.

   k. No meat.

   l. Organic fruits and vegetables.

   m. Turmeric, blueberries, seaweed, Chia seeds, vitamin C, apple cider vinegar and green mix (Spirulina, wheatgrass, buckwheat grass, chlorella).

   n. No processed foods.

   o. Avoid alcohol, sugar, tobacco and caffeine.

   p. Spring water.

   q. No fluoride, chlorine or bromide.

CLEARING THE PINEAL GLAND

In today's world there's a lot of fluoride and chlorine in many things. Both fluoride and chlorine calcify our pineal gland – so do try to avoid fluoride and chlorine as much as possible.

Here are suggestions for avoiding fluoride:

Tap water is the biggest culprit. Don't drink it or cook with it. There are in-house systems for filtering fluoride (reverse osmosis), but they may be expensive. If you're just starting out, you may not want to support that expense, but you can do your best to avoid drinking tap water.

When buying bottled water, remember that a lot of purified water has fluoride in it. Purchase spring water, and if you can purchase one with alkaline in it, that's even better. Toothpaste is another product with fluoride, so look for toothpaste without fluoride. Why? Because avoiding products with fluoride helps the third eye. Although, I know it is best not to use fluoride, I will leave that to your discretion. I will tell you to go within and ask yourself. If you have ever met me or seen a picture of me, you know I have a big smile with big teeth. I like my teeth and smile. I have extremely sensitive teeth and have used several non-fluoride toothpastes.

We can't avoid these things completely, but we can drastically reduce them. Other things that calcify the pineal gland include sodas, artificial drinks, red meats, non-organic fruits and vegetables, sugar, alcohol and caffeine. <u>Calcification can be removed over time. The items on the list below can help you speed up your calcification removal.</u>

* **Organic Blue Ice Skate Fish Oil:** <u>This is useful for non-vegetarians</u>. You can buy it in a capsule. It's a form of fish liver oil and rich in Vitamins A, D, E, and K – the full range of omega fatty acids, plus the unique nutrients chondroitin, squalene, and alkoxglycerols. Naturally, if you're a vegetarian, it's not recommended.

* **MSM** (methylsulfonylmethane) is a supplement used to lower inflammation. It's organic sulfur and contains a compound that helps arthritic pain. It does soften the pineal gland.

* **Raw Chocolate** Don't get too excited. Raw chocolate is a minimally processed food and considered a super food. I remember when my mom used baking chocolate it tasted really bad because it had no sugar or fat. Yes, that's raw chocolate! Make sure you get RAW chocolate. No other will do. Don't cheat and add sugar or anything else, because that calcifies it.

* **Citric Acid** This one's easy. Just add lemons, oranges, etc. to your water. Lemons are best, and remember to use the spring water we talked about earlier.

* **Garlic, raw apple cider vinegar, oregano oil and Neem extract** are also helpful.

* **Melatonin** is natural, inexpensive, and easy to find.

* **Iodine** Purchase liquid iodine and add a couple drops of it to water. This helps decalcify the pineal gland. I found in my research that a lot of people add sulfur to this mixture. MSM (organic sulfur) can be added, and distilled water is recommended – but be aware that iodine does strip

your body of calcium, so you want to avoid this practice if you're low on calcium.

OTHER RECOMMENDATIONS:

Imagination – Your imagination can get you in touch with your inner child. Daydream. Laugh uncontrollably! As one of my mentors says, "Don't take life so seriously. Take your soul seriously – but not life!"

She is right. *Have fun!* This world presents us with challenges to help us grow. This we all know and experience, but there's no reason why we can't also enjoy a great deal of fun – so quit taking your self so seriously. Consider what your inner eight-year-old thinks about you. As adults we do face responsibilities, must work to pay bills and put food on the table – but by golly, why not have fun doing it? Make it a primary goal to play as much as possible. Just give it a try. For the next three months, concentrate on having fun!

Be Creative – Do something creative: painting, coloring, writing, drawing, yoga, etc. Do it with the intention of getting in touch with inspiration. Do it to have fun! With that fun you will express your feelings and emotions. Who cares if the drawing you make is not perfect? If you have always wanted to paint go to a group paint-night or just purchase cheap paints and play with them. Here the phrase 'Just do it' does fit. So do not hold back – go for it! (You'll be glad you did.)

You may look at the above list and say, 'I understand the third eye information, but what does getting in touch with my inner child and being creative have to do with psychic abilities?'

My emphatic answer is, 'Everything!' When we were children we were intuitive because we were open. As we matured we created blocks, judgments and barriers that stopped our energy flow. That's why we are not allowing ourselves to fully express who we are. The first two suggestions on this list (Imagination and Be Creative) can be described as "spirited" suggestions. Our aim is to become whole, to know again our inner child – so we can be a responsible adult and wise seeker.

It is crucial that we each learn to understand our flow of energy and how we can balance that energy, for when it's balanced we understand ourselves better. When we can understand and control our own energy, we can also control the energy others express in our presence or toward us. Reaching the point of understanding the energy flow enables us to act rather than react in any situation.

Next time you look in the mirror, take a moment to really look at yourself. Realize that what you are staring at is not you. *You* are the light within you. *You* are your God-self.

You have always been that, though perhaps you've never really acknowledged it. You are the Light. Right now, at this moment, you are commanding trillions of cells and microorganisms. They form the body you have identified as you, and that body is temporary. You're commanding your own universe, even if you haven't known you are. Imagine what you can do, now that you are aware and awakened.

Be the beacon of light – and shine. Your Light may be what someone else requires to find his or her way. Until then, be kind and love each other.

CPSIA information can be obtained
at www.ICGtesting.com
Printed in the USA
LVHW080452191219
641008LV00004B/65/P